19,

D1635970

Winning the Job Interview Game
New Strategies for Getting Hired

Bruce R. Hammond, Ph.D.

LIBERTY HALL
PRESS™

To June for her encouraging love, and to
John and Vanessa for years of quiet understanding.

LIBERTY HALL PRESS books are published by LIBERTY HALL PRESS, a division of TAB BOOKS. Its trademark, consisting of the words "LIBERTY HALL PRESS" and the portrayal of Benjamin Franklin, is registered in the United States Patent and Trademark Office.

First Edition
First Printing

©1990 by TAB BOOKS
Printed in the United States of America

Library of Congress Cataloging-in-Publication Data

Hammond, Bruce R.
  Winning the job interview game: new strategies for getting hired
/ by Bruce R. Hammond.
    p.   cm.
  ISBN 0-8306-3505-X
  1. Employment interviewing. I. Title.
HF5549.5.I6H34 1990
650.14—dc20   90-5716
                                                                          CIP

TAB BOOKS. offers software for sale.
For information and a catalog, please contact:

TAB Software Department
Blue Ridge Summit, PA 17294-0850

Questions regarding the content of this book
should be addressed to:

Reader Inquiry Branch
Division of TAB BOOKS
Blue Ridge Summit, PA 17294-0214

Acquisitions Editor: David J. Conti
Book Editor: Molly Jackel
Production: Katherine G. Brown

Cover photograph by Brent Blair, Harrisburg, PA.

Contents

Introduction

THROUGH THE YEARS, I HAVE HAD MORE JOBS THAN I CAN POSSIBLY remember or count. I have been everything from a garbage man to an engineer, from a taxi driver to a college professor. Quite simply, I have had very broad experience in many fields calling for a wide variety of backgrounds and skills.

Curiously, most of these jobs have had very little in common except for one thing; in nearly every case, the interview for the job was a joke. It was generally informal, unstructured, random and based on the interviewer's personal feelings rather than facts. And, as often as not, the interviewer was an absolutely untrained person who had no idea of how to conduct an interview. After a time, I came to understand that the employment interview was a game, and like every other game, if you know the rules and the techniques needed to play, you have a much better chance of winning. That is what this book is all about. It will teach you the rules of the game and prepare you to play the game like an expert. For instance, *Winning the Job Interview Game* gives you methods for dealing with the most difficult questions and it provides sample answers that will overcome nearly any obstacle. It presents effective suggestions for designing resumes and handling yourself while setting up an appointment. It even suggests ways to "read" the interviewer in order to give him or her what he or she wants. In short, it provides a complete recipe for you that will work again and again. This is because the book deals in reality and presents practical advice based on my years of direct interviewing experience both as the interviewer and the interviewee. It also reflects thousands of hours of research in the field including interviews with human resource or personnel managers and college recruiters.

Although other books on the subject may make the same claims, in one way or another they all come up short. There are many reasons for this. First, it has been my unhappy experience to discover that most books on the subject do not give you a very realistic picture of what is going on out there. For instance, they will tell you to "act naturally" and "relax" when that is precisely what you should not do. There is, after all, nothing natural or relaxing about an employment interview. In fact, it is a conflict-ridden situation where you are determined to win the job, and the employer is determined not to consider you unless you are exactly what he wants. To act naturally (respond to his or her questions with the first thing that pops into your brain and say anything you please about everything) or relax (sit there in a comfortable position casually watching him or her talk) would not only be a mistake, it would be stupid.

Also, most other books on employment interviewing will tell you that the employer is more interested in your skills than anything else, which is simply not true. Employers assume that you have the same basic skills as the others they are interviewing or they would not have bothered talking to you in the first place. What they are really looking for is a good personality mix; they want to know if you will fit into the organization without conflict and strain. At this point, how you act and what you look like is much more important than your exact level of skill.

Second, most other books of this sort are written by people who know the theory but have not tested or lived through the reality of the employment interviewing experience. They are often well-intentioned personnel veterans who have never really understood the process, or they tend to be academics who will tell you the way it should be rather than the way it really is. To make matters worse, these unrealistic ideas about employment interviewing are often reinforced by well-meaning teachers, guidance counselors, or friends. They assume it is a logical and scientific process. However, this is rarely the case.

Other books aside, your own direct experience may not coincide with what is presented in this book. So, in order for the book to prove valuable, you have to accept that I know what I am talking about, even if it negates what has personally happened to you. Given this fact, you will probably find the material uncomfortable, at first, but as you think about the ideas and suggestions, I know that you will find them sound in the long run. Certainly, once you have had the opportunity to put the book to use, you will be happily surprised to find that it works. It is, in the final analysis, a cookbook with recipes for finding a job. If you follow the proven methods presented here (the recipes), you will get exactly the same results that I have when I used them myself.

The immediate benefits will be considerable. You will find that you get more job interview offers. You will discover that you have more confidence in such situations. You will notice that you are better prepared for the unexpected. You will negotiate more effectively and win your point more often. Finally, following the guidelines will lessen the stress and tension that you will feel. Of course, if you vary the methods or ignore the book, you can expect varied results.

My advice to you is simple. Read the book, think long and carefully about the material presented rather than rejecting it immediately and then use the material to find a job, taking each step literally; if you do, you will soon find that you will be employed in the job you want. You will have played the interview game, and won! And with that victory will come the benefits that are a part of the process.

In any case, no matter how experienced or well educated you are, this book will work for you. No matter what level of job you are looking for, the methods presented here will prove effective. The graduating high school senior and the experienced executive can both use the book to great advantage. Whether you have been let go from a prominent position, or you are deliberately making a career change, it can make a significant impact on your efforts to find the position that you want. This is because the rules of the employment interviewing game do not really change, and once you have read the book you will be one of the fortunate minority who truly understands them.

I wish you success and I know that this book can help you land the job that you want.

1

Why the System
Can Be Beat

SOME YEARS AGO, I WAS DESPERATELY LOOKING FOR A SUMMER job. I was between my junior and senior years in college and, without work, I would not have been able to return to school in the fall. I had been watching the newspapers for about two weeks when I noticed an ad for a management trainee for a retail chain. It read:

> Management Trainee needed for national retail organization. We offer extensive training with excellent benefits and excellent potential. We require a candidate with at least 2 years of college and demonstrated ambition. For an interview, report to _____ in the Central Park Plaza, 8 AM, Monday, May 10. No phone calls, please.

Because I needed the job so badly, I made sure I was there at 6:30—an hour and a half early. But when I arrived I discovered a lot of other people had the same thought. There were at least twenty-five others standing in a long line in front of the closed store.

At this time, by the way, jobs were scarce because the American economy was in a recession. If you were lucky enough to find a job, you kept it. Under the circumstances, I should have guessed there would be a line but I was depressed, anyway. "How," I thought, "could I possibly get the job with all those others applying?" I felt like walking away.

Still, I had no real choice in the matter so, I remained there with the others. My mind kept telling me that my education and career were at stake and that my life in general, in a very real sense, depended on getting that job. This was, after all, the only real opportunity advertised in the newspapers for weeks. So, I glumly waited as more and more people lined up behind me. By 8:00 AM at least forty others joined us.

Eventually, the door opened and they began letting people into the dark store, five at a time. When it was my group's turn to be let inside, we were led to the back of the store, told to stand against a wall outside the employees' lounge, and fill out applications. Then, one at a time, each of the people in front of me entered the room to be questioned by three personnel executives from New York City.

The door of the lounge remained open during each of these interviews, and I could easily hear everything that was being said. I remember that I was struck by the fact that the questions I overheard seemed almost random, off-handed. But there was one common thread to many of them; the candidates were always asked, in one way or another, how much money they wanted to earn that year.

Eventually, it was my turn and I was absolutely terrified. Everything was on the line and I began to search desperately for something to make me stand out, to look just different enough to be the one hired.

The three executives were sitting at a round table and they told me to take a chair some feet away. They seemed smug, self-important, and even arrogant in their dark, three-piece suits. My sense of inadequacy deepened.

"Have you had any management experience?" asked the one holding my application.

"No," I muttered.

"Any retail experience?" another wanted to know.

"Ah . . . no, I'm afraid not."

"Why should we hire you?" The first one demanded.

Now, for some reason I can't explain even today, I blurted out, "Money."

"What?" someone asked.

"Money!" I answered more strongly. "Money! Anyone who hires me is going to make money because that's what I am all about." At this point, I don't think I knew what I was talking about but I was on a roll.

"What do you mean?" A thin, very surprised face inquired.

I continued on my improvised theme. "I intend to make a lot of money and the only way that's going to happen is if I make money for you by working hard and producing." I stopped abruptly, nearly exhausted from my short but outrageous fiction.

One of the interviewers suddenly stood up, walked hurriedly over to me, and shook my hand. "Gentlemen," he exclaimed, "this fellow is our kind of people. I say that we don't have to look any further. He's our man!" he said with gusto and enthusiasm.

I was hired on the spot and the remaining candidates were told to go home. It was probably the most bizarre business moment of my life.

I've thought about the strange interview a lot over the years and have analyzed the dynamics of it at least a hundred times. I'll never be sure, of course, but it seems that my subconscious mind was locked in on what they *wanted* to hear and I just gave it to them. Whatever it was, the situation was unstructured, essentially unplanned by the interviewers, and it allowed me to control the results.

Incidentally, this interview occurred more than 20 years ago. You would think that things would have changed by now and that the process of hiring people would be more scientific. But oddly enough, it is still essentially the same today as it was then. As a recruiter and consultant in this area for some of the largest companies in the country, I can personally attest to the fact that, with rare exception, most positions (even the high paying ones), are filled in this haphazard way.

Such interviews, of course, allow the candidate to take over by answering his or her way, by picking and choosing what he or she wants and has to say, and by twisting and turning questions to his or her own ends. The bottom line is that if you play the game right, you win. *You get the job.* If you don't play the game, no matter how well qualified you are on paper, you don't get the job. It is not a matter of training or experience, then, as much as it is the way you look and sound. Oh, the education and background that you have is important, but only to the point that it gets you the interview in the first place. After that, it becomes less and less a factor in being hired.

In the face of all this, it stands to reason that the person who prepares answers in advance, and projects the right physical image, has a better than ever chance of beating the system and landing the position he or she wants.

You might be asking yourself at this point whether or not the interviewer can really be as easily manipulated as I have implied, and if so why? Well, first of all, very few employment interviewers have ever had any formal training in the process. Second, it is widely assumed (with very little scientific evidence to support it) that informal, relatively unstructured interviews bring out the "real candidate" and allow the employer to discover the "true" person. Third, most interviewers make up questions as they go or use hackneyed cliche questions. And fourth, very few of them have any other model from which to work. In other words, that is the way they were questioned during their own interviews as candidates, and they simply don't know any other way to do it.

It goes without saying that in situations like this, the employer often loses. The manager hires a person who might or might not be appropriate to the job and hopes for the best. The candidate might also lose if he or she doesn't know what is going on in the situation. My own experience tells me that nine out of ten times both parties lose under these circumstances. That is too bad because there are valid ways to truly qualify people. For now, though, you probably are concerned with landing the job rather than making sure the employer gets what he or she wants.

The popular system of employment interviewing can be overcome because it is no system at all. Few employers have the necessary safeguards to prevent you from getting the job that you want.

Take the case of a very attractive woman from the Midwest who responded to an advertisement for a management job with a major hotel chain. Her only experience up to that point was as a social worker in Chicago. She found herself burned out and the new position in question attracted her because it was so different from what she was doing. It apparently did not bother her that she lacked the proper training or experience. In any case, she applied for the job and despite the odds, she got it. Today, she is one of the highest paid and most powerful executives in the company. It was a lucky break for her and the company to be sure, but certainly not typical of most employment interview outcomes. Everything points to the fact that she was hired because she looked and sounded good to the man who first talked to her. It certainly was not a question of being qualified!

I once became a shoe salesman because, when I was interviewed by the store manager, he asked, "Do you know much about shoes?"

"Yes," I replied.

"Have you had much experience in shoes?" he went on.

"Sure, a number of years," I answered.

"Well," he said, "I guess we'll give you a try."

I must confess that my answers to his questions were based on the fact that I had been wearing shoes all of my life. I had never sold them, of course, but then he never really asked me that.

This illustration points out another reality of the employment interviewing process. Most employers seldom check on the candidate's background. It might seem crazy, but in my experience with most companies—even Fortune 500 companies—background checks are routinely ignored. Partly, this is because if they really want you, they do not want to learn anything negative that could possibly spoil their plans. Also, in many cases, it is simply a question of thinking someone else in the organization has already done it. Finally, some recruiters are just too lazy to bother. As a candidate, once again, it is to your benefit because there might be things about your previous employment you would rather not discuss.

To summarize, you can beat the employment interview if you follow the basic principles presented in the chapters that follow. Remember, most interviews are unplanned, unstructured, and highly subjective regarding looks and feelings. In such a setting, the candidate can take charge and manipulate the interview.

The remainder of this book, then, is a step-by-step blueprint on how to prepare yourself for the employment interview that stands in your way of becoming whatever you want to be. It provides everything from simple suggestions on discovering what your prospective employer is really looking for, to answers to those standard questions that nearly every recruiter asks. It also gives numerous examples of how even the most unqualified people have wound up in important, responsible, high-paying jobs. Finally, it offers information on where to locate the best jobs, and it highlights ways to deal with the special problems that you might encounter.

It might seem that getting that good job you want just has to be harder than this book outlines and that it is too good to be true. It is not. Believe me, it is probably easier to get the job you want than you think.

2

Getting Started

BEFORE YOU GET TO THE ACTUAL INTERVIEW STAGE, THERE ARE A number of things you must consider.

First, you must convince the employer to see you. Normally, this is done by sending in a resume to an address listed in a newspaper. Or it may be that you have given it to an employment agency to forward for you. However you handle it, the resume must generate interest in you. It must *sell* you.

Now, as a rule, the shorter the resume the better. Most of my colleagues in the recruiting field follow a basic principle: if the resume is more than one page, put it aside. Bear in mind, of course, that you can include a lot on one page if you know what you are doing.

You should start by recognizing that some things about you are simply unimportant. Take, for example, the fact that you were president of your Home Economics club in high school. Or that you were once given a special Boy Scout medal for flying an airplane. Employers are rarely interested in such trivia, no matter how significant it is to you.

Then there is the point that some information can actually hurt you. I had one candidate-client I was advising who insisted on including in his resume that he was a Presbyterian Deacon. This would be fine if the potential employer was a Presbyterian as well, but that possibility is so remote, it can't seriously be considered.

What my client failed to recognize is that some employers are bigotted and might not bring you in for an interview because you are a member of the "wrong" religion. As a rule, then, avoid putting anything in your resume that can be used against you and prejudice your chances of landing the job. The following resume, as you will see, violates these principles.

ED BLAKE

1423 University Blvd.   Birmingham, AL   412-711-7006

EDUCATION	University of Alabama BA 1978 Majored in English 3.4 GPA
	Parker H.S., Birmingham, AL 1974 College Prep 95 average
	Ellenville Elementary School, Birmingham, AL 1970
EXPERIENCE	Doblin Industries: Assistant Prod. Mgr., Familiar with C.D.L. units, Prep systems, supervised 2 clerks, 1978 to present
	Parker Drugs: stock boy, clerk, 1977 to 1978
	Ed's Garage: mechanics helper, 1976 to 1977
	Catholic Youth Camp: Assistant Counselor, 1975 (summer)
MEMBERSHIPS	Young Catholic Executives Club Rotary Club (Northside) Alpha Kappa Psi Sky Divers of Birmingham, Inc.
HOBBIES	Sky diving Tournament Chess (1st Degree) Karate Master, 3rd degree black belt

It should be obvious that the resume has some very serious flaws. Take, for example, that Mr. Blake used "Ed" in the heading rather than Edward. This is much too informal and could easily lead to the impression that the candidate is frivolous or flippant. Job hunting is a serious business and the resume should reflect that seriousness. Most employers I deal with would automatically reject a resume that begins with a nickname.

In the education section, our hapless composer has made several errors. First, if you have a college degree, there is no reason to include any other schooling unless it demonstrates professional skill or training. If your highest formal education ended with high school, then you should omit the elementary school you attended. Including all but the most significant educational experiences makes the writer look foolish. It's as though he or she is desperate to impress the reader so he or she tries to include everything.

Second, we know he graduated with a Bachelor of Arts degree and that he majored in English. But all of that doesn't mean much to the prospective employer. It doesn't tell him how an English major qualifies him for business life. Most people would probably assume many wrong things, such as, that he studied Shakespeare to the exclusion of business writing, or that all he knows is poetry or theatre. It would be much better to specify course work related to business or management such as report writing, communication, psychology, advertising, etc. As it stands, the resume tells us little about his training.

Finally, in this section the writer has made the mistake of including his college grade-point, or quality-point, average. In this case, the average is quite high, indicating a low "A" or high "B." One might assume that a high average in college would be a plus, but, many executives would be put off by this because it constitutes a threat.

As strange as this may seem, an extremely bright or accomplished person scares most employers at first, because this makes them feel less intelligent or talented. It might be a source of pride for the candidate, but can represent a serious threat to his or her chances of being interviewed. It makes sense to simply omit any reference to grades. You can always bring this up if necessary.

In the experience section, the writer has made additional mistakes. For one thing, it makes him look like he has jumped from job to job. Close inspection indicates, of course, that this isn't the case; Mr. Blake worked at at part time jobs while going to school.

Such jobs are rarely stable and are frequently subject to the vagaries of school pressures and economics. But the busy person doing the resume screening might eliminate the candidate for this reason alone. So it is best to include only those serious, full time jobs you have had.

For another thing, the writer has described his professional activities with terms that aren't familiar to the layperson. What is a "C.D.L. Unit" or a "Prep System?" As most people know, in any job you use terms, phrases, and alphabets that are peculiar to that company or industry. It is natural for any of us to forget that the general public (even someone in the same business) may not understand what we are talking about. What it really comes down to is that these terms don't clarify what we can do, and don't give the employer any particular reason to see us. It is much better to detail your skill experience and job-related knowledge in generic terms so that they become familiar to the person screening the resume.

Finally, in this section the writer has indicated he supervises two clerks. Now, anyone who thinks carefully about supervision is aware that the same basic principles apply whether you are controlling one or a dozen workers. In short, the candidate has apparently learned the rudiments of supervision through direct experience no matter how many people he has been working with. Admitting that he supervises just two people makes him sound somewhat inexperienced and possibly amateurish. It would be much better to say that he has been in supervision and then list his many responsibilities. It is not a question of lying; it is a question of maximizing your assets.

But perhaps our candidate's biggest error is in the next section where he lists his hobbies. As I said earlier, many prospective employers are very prejudiced when it comes to religious or even fraternal organizations. Beyond this, the candidate's reference to being a sky diver and martial arts enthusiast proclaims that he is a big risk taker and this alone could disqualify him from being hired. Now, as if this weren't enough, he has indicated he is a first degree tournament chess player that would absolutely terrify some employers. This brings us back to the point that you don't include anything in a resume that will bias your case. It becomes a question of creating a document that impresses rather than bothers or threatens the potential employer.

However, the resume is only one initial part of what you must do to gain the job you want. After you have sent the resume to the employer, it is imperative to find out as much about the company as possible. There are a number of ways to do this.

First, you can contact the company in advance and ask for their annual report. As odd as it seems, they will often send this to you without question. In this report is a wealth of information about the corporate culture (its general business philosophy), its profitability, and its potential for growth. This same type of information is also available in the public library.

Second, you can always ask your friends or associates what they know about the company. They might be familiar with the operation or they might even know the person who is going to interview you.

Third, the administrative assistant who arranges the interview will frequently tell you about the position, even about his or her boss; but, you must ask. If you can't get the administrative assistant to divulge anything at the time he or she is setting up the interview, once you arrive at the office, you can ask him or her questions such as:

> "Is this a new position or will the candidate be replacing someone?"
> "How long has Mr./Ms. _ _ _ _ _ _ _ _ _ (the interviewer) been with the company?"
> "What is it like to work for the _ _ _ _ _ _ _ _ Company?"
> "Is this an entry level position?"
> "Have they interviewed many people for this job?"
> "Who is in the position now?"

All of these questions will provide a significant amount of information for the candidate. And the administrative assistant will usually be flattered that you are asking his or her advice or opinion. Of course, why he or she gives you the information you need is less important than the fact that you can get vital data that you can use to your advantage.

The first question, for instance, will tell you whether the position has built-in expectations because of a current success or failure. It might also tell you why the position is available and its level of significance to the organization.

The second question can give you a fairly good idea of the kind of person who will be interviewing you. Is he or she a new person with points to make in the company? Is he or she someone with a great deal of or very little interviewing experience? Is he or she someone who has a deep allegiance to the company or a person who is more interested in impressing you with his or her power?

When you ask the administrative assistant what it is like to work for the company, he or she might give you an earful of suggestions and opinions. I once asked an administrative assistant this question and she said that the company was "O.K., but they kind of work you to death!" She laughed but that didn't hide her sincerity. Then she continued, "Don't get me wrong. I love working here but you better be willing to put in a lot of overtime. That job, in particular, is a real pressure cooker."

Even if the administrative assistant is reluctant, or downright unwilling, to answer these and other questions, there are still more ways of getting useful information about the company. The public library can give you historical and financial information and other pertinent factors regarding such things as the founding of the company, its philosophy, and its general track record. *The Wall Street Journal*, *Fortune Magazine*, *The New York Times*, among others, are excellent sources for information about companies.

Finally, there is no substitute for talking with a friend, or an acquaintance, who works for the organization. While this might be a rare opportunity at best, and will occur only occasionally, it can be worth its weight in gold. More specifically, a friend can counsel you on advantages and disadvantages, suggest approaches, tell you who and what to avoid, and even when it might be best to make the initial contact with the company.

The message should be clear. The more you know about the organization, the better prepared you will be for the interview and the greater chance you will have of getting the job. It will give you the edge that can make the difference. If the interviewer asks you if you want to join a corporation in order to get ahead (move from promotion to promotion), you will have a better idea of whether to say yes or no. If the interviewer asks you whether you consider yourself a "team player or an individualist," you can answer more effectively if you know the type of person he or she is looking for. Or, if the interviewer asks you about your background (i.e. "Why did you decide to become an accounting major?"), you will be able to answer best if you have done your homework.

Curiously, only a small portion of candidates that I have interviewed over the years have bothered to research the organization I was representing. One classic example was the gentleman I was interviewing a few years ago. The position I was trying to fill was a vice-president of operations for a company deeply involved in a "Management by Objectives" (M.B.O.) program which centered on high accountability and control. Presumably, anyone applying for this position, at this level, would at least be familiar with the system.

When I asked the man what he knew about the process he answered, "I've seen your signs."

"What?" I asked.

"I've seen your signs everywhere."

At this point I should explain that the initials of the company were M.O.S.

"No," I explained, "I'm afraid you misunderstood my question. What I wanted to know was what do you think of Management By Objectives as a system?"

"Well," he answered nervously, "I really like it."

"Why?" I pressed.

"It helps you . . . ah . . . understand the marketplace."

"Thank you," I responded, and I abruptly dismissed the man. As you might or might not know, M.B.O. has little to do with the "the marketplace" as he put it. So the candidate eliminated himself because he didn't understand what the company was doing. If he had done his background research, he would have been able to answer the question easily. Every person in the company, including the receptionist, was keenly aware of the impact of the program on the organization. A simple question to her would have given him the edge he needed.

In an extreme situation in which you cannot find anything in the library, or the company won't divulge anything about itself, it might still be possible to go to the offices of the organization and look at their operation from the inside or outside.

Even the exterior of the building can give you clues about its conservative or liberal posture. For instance, a slick glass and steel building with modern furniture suggests a more dynamic, risk-taking philosophy, whereas a stately brick and wooden structure may demonstrate a more careful approach to business. It is no accident that the most creative, high-tech organizations look like the work they do; modern architecture, sculptured furniture, and plastic surfaces. Then, there is the bank in the major southern city that has its headquarters in a renovated, 19th century, downtown landmark. It has also been decorated in 19th century furnishings. The bank, as you might guess, is very conservative and very slow to react to any situation.

Now that you know something about the organizations that you may want to join, it becomes a question of applying your knowledge to its best advantage.

The best way to begin is to memorize answers to questions you can expect to be asked. The following is an abbreviated list of typical questions that will serve you well if you are prepared to answer them:

"Why did you decide to become an accountant?"
"Why do you want to work for the West End Pressure Tank Company?"
"What qualifications do you possess that will help you in this job?"
"How do you feel about travel?"
"What do you know about our company?"
"Why did you leave your last job?"
"What are your personal plans and ambitions?"
"How do you spend your spare time?"
"What are your professional goals as far as this company is concerned?"

Now, if you look at each of the questions you will discover that they are all open-ended and subjective. That is, they ask for answers that you can usually shape to your own ends.

For example, "Why did you decide to become an accountant?" should be answered with a response that is committed to memory, based on your research. Let us suppose that the company in question is a small, well-established manufacturing firm that specializes in high-pressure tanks. The firm is well-known for quality and its reputation is built on years of service to its customers. Let us further suppose that it has a few steady contracts that amount to 90% of its yearly sales.

A company like this would probably want a straight-forward accountant who would treat any customer (even the most irate and rude customer) with extreme politeness and who would exhibit a strong sense of public relations. They would also want a team player, one who follows orders and doesn't rock the boat with radical ideas and new ways of doing things. Finally, they would probably subscribe to the notion that "if it isn't broken, don't fix it."

If a person has done his or her basic research, he or she should know his or her response to the question, "Why did you decide to become an accountant?" It should sound something like the following:

"Well, sir, I decided on accounting because it is a service position that supports operations. It demands a person who enjoys helping others achieve goals. And, perhaps above all, the best accountants are a vital part of a team effort. As far as I am concerned, working with others is enjoyable but more to the point, it is a satisfying way of making a contribution to the total effort."

If the interviewer followed up with "Why do you want to work for the West End Pressure Tank Corporation?" the proper response, under the circumstances would be as follows:

"As I'm sure you know, West End enjoys a solid reputation in this area as a high quality manufacturer that doesn't compromise on anything. And that's the kind of company for which I want to work. There are a lot of fast-track organizations that look good on the outside but who don't respect the tradition of craftsmanship and respect for the customer that you do. As I'm sure you know, West End stands out in this regard."

You may be saying to yourself, no interviewer in his or her right mind would ever fall for such a line. Fortunately for the interviewee, most of those asking the questions do fall for such answers. You see, so few of them are trained in interviewing, and so many of them hear such ineffective and half-baked answers, that anything sounding articulate and well thought out, stands out as a pleasant and well-received response. Most candidates, asked the same questions, will hesitate and stumble through their answers.

It is not uncommon to hear foolish answers like:

"Well, I thought I'd . . . uh . . . become an accountant because I . . . well, I was always kind of good at figures and it seemed like a good idea . . . especially for a guy who likes to work alone, ha, ha!"

I have personally heard the following answer to the question, "Why do you want to work for the _ _ _ _ _ _ _ _ _ Company?"

"Uh . . . I've been shopping around. I don't know. I thought this might be a good opportunity."

Another classic response went as follows:

"To be perfectly honest, I'm not sure I want to work for your company. I just saw your ad so I thought that I'd apply. Besides, I'm looking at another company that looks pretty good."

It is hard to imagine why someone would apply for a job without really wanting to work for the particular company, especially when he or she hardly knew anything about the nature of the position or the opportunity it presented. Perhaps it was a question of not knowing what else to say. Nevertheless, the memorized, structured, and well-planned response to these questions is superior because it will make a better impression than the stumbling, sometimes ridiculous and self-defeating answers frequently presented.

The rehearsed responses are impressive because they tell the interviewer that: you took the time to research the company; you are very articulate and therefore very able; and most important, you sound good.

However, even the best speech is useless unless you look the part as well. In other words, you must dress and act appropriately or your words will hardly be heard. If you think about it, we all see people in interviews before we hear them. Before the first syllable, the employer will notice clothing, grooming, and body movements. Let's begin with the way you dress.

It has been established that people tend to hire *themselves* over and over again. That's because it is only natural to want to work with those who think, look, and act the same way we do. Therefore, if at all possible, the person doing the hiring will "clone" him or herself, or hire a look-alike everytime he or she has a chance.

It stands to reason, then, that you should try to dress for an interview with an eye toward imitating the person conducting it. In the banking business, for instance, most middle and upper-management men wear dark, three piece suits with a conservative necktie, button-down shirt, and wing-tip shoes. Upper management women tend to dress equally conservatively; on the other hand, in many sales positions, a dark blue blazer, contrasting tan pants, and brown loafers is perfectly acceptable.

Then, there is the question of jewelry. The best idea is to wear as little as possible. I once knew a man who refused to hire an excellent candidate because he was wearing a gold "pinkie" ring. A college ring is universally acceptable, but a "pinkie" ring can prevent a person from getting hired! Even a lapel pin can get you in trouble. If you are a member of one civic or fraternal organization, you might offend an employer who belongs to another.

A woman wearing anything more than very small, simple earrings, and one conservative ring, is risking getting the job she is after. She might appear too "flashy," or "feminine" to the interviewer.

On the other hand, you can't dress too formally for an interview. This contention is based on the idea that people tend to respect those who dress formally and this, in turn, almost always translates to a favorable impression even if the job itself is casual. A case in point is the college junior who once approached me about getting a job as a bartender. He felt confident, he said, except that he needed some advice about what to wear for the interview.

"What kind of place is it?" I asked.

"It's a college hangout. Nothing fancy," he replied.

"My advice," I said, "is to go to the interview in a three-piece suit."

"You don't understand," he explained. "It's a really casual place. They don't even wear uniforms."

"That may be," I responded. "But if you do what I suggest, you'll look more serious than the other applicants who dress down, and I'll bet you'll stand out from the crowd."

He was reluctant, at first, but I convinced him. To his happy surprise, he got the job despite the fact that he had no previous experience as a bartender and others who had applied for the job did. Several months later, he asked his boss why he had been hired instead of someone else; the response was:

"The first and most basic reason was that you looked better than the other guys. You were the only one who looked serious. I guess I was impressed by your suit."

I have heard this story repeated time and again. As strange as it may seem, it is almost impossible to dress too formally for an interview.

Personally, I find it astonishing that people show up in the strange costumes that they do for employment interviews. Once, when I was trying to hire a branch manager for a collection agency, one man walked in wearing a cowboy outfit complete with everything but spurs and a holster. He even kept his cowboy hat on during our discussion. As you might surmise, it was a short interview. Another time, when I was seeking a middle manager for a small bank, a man came into my office in designer jeans and a velvet blazer. And in another situation, a candidate for a position as project engineer for a hazardous waste disposal company turned up in dirty clothes and a hardhat. Although he explained that he had come directly from work, the fact that he was greasy and was soiling my office furniture and left an oily imprint on my hand when we shook hands didn't exactly impress me. In fact, although he was qualified on paper, he disqualified himself by walking in filthy.

Then, there is the question of looking too good. A very attractive woman came into my office wearing a red sundress that was held together at each shoulder by two buttons. Each side had one button that was undone, and I spent my time wondering whether or not the whole dress would fall down. My concentration was further diverted by her very exposed cleavage. I didn't seriously consider her for the job in question because she looked too sexy and not much like an executive. The strange thing was that her credentials were extremely impressive and I was convinced, before I saw her, that she could do the job. She may have been very capable but the way she dressed, coupled with her obvious attempts to charm me with her figure, turned me off. In fact, it made me angry.

It may seem to the reader that I was being shallow and arbitrary in dismissing these candidates on the basis of appearances alone; but, in my experience, and in the bulk of research on the topic, people tend to reflect themselves in their clothing. A collection agency doesn't want a pseudo-cowboy managing it's operation and a bank doesn't want or need a playboy handling its funds. By the same token, a project engineer for a hazardous waste company has to be concerned with details and a person who carelessly leaves grease and oil stains behind is hardly the meticulous type. In any case, arbitrary or not, every employment interviewer I have known tends to judge people based on their appearance. So it is up to the candidate to look right. Looking right, however, is more than wearing the right clothes. It is also a matter of proper grooming. Studies demonstrate that people are inherently prejudice against those who have extreme hair styles, dirty nails, or unpleasant odors. You can be a genius with the most impeccable references and still not land the job because of one of the offenses listed above.

Ask yourself the following question. If you had two acceptable men to consider for a job, each with identical credentials, and one of them had a pony tail and the other had well-trimmed hair, which one would you pick? Research tells us that unless you are very unusual, you would pick the man with the trimmed hair. Naturally, it depends to some extent on the specific position, but it would be rare to choose otherwise.

Once I was asked to talk with a potential vice-president of finance for a large, independently-owned department store. The owner was a client of mine and I had helped him recruit management personnel at other levels. The candidate had met my client at a cocktail party and apparently impressed him in some way. At his request, I saw the man in my office, and although he was a mature businessman with considerable executive experience, his fingernails were a disgrace with ends black with dirt. Also, his necktie was stained and his shoes had mud spots on them. Small items, to be sure, but they added up to an alarming picture for a man in a profession allegedly concerned with details. On top of this, vice-president of finance he would be expected to set an example for his staff. My recommendation to my client was not to hire him, for the reasons that I have mentioned. He was hired, nonetheless, and I was told it was just a question of having him "clean up his act." Apparently, my client spoke to him about his appearance.

For the first month or so, everything was fine. But before long, he returned to his old habits and, in time, after repeated warnings about his sloppy appearance, he was fired. Eventually, the owner conceded to me that the general discipline of his whole department began to suffer and that the vice-president's appearance was just a small part of his "sloppiness problem."

So it pays to look your best particularly when someone is looking you over as a potential employee. You can argue that drawing conclusions on the basis of something like appearance is "unfair." But it is a reality that you can expect.

3

Locating the Job

As YOU MIGHT IMAGINE, MOST PEOPLE TURN TO THE NEWSPAPER to find a job; however, there are many other avenues that the individual can explore. In this chapter, we will examine each job location possibility and determine their potential value in a job search. We will start with the newspaper.

THE NEWSPAPER

The typical classified section of the newspaper categorizes jobs according to the skill, training, or experience needed. For example, one large Florida newspaper uses the following headings: administrative; accounting/bookkeeping; clerical/secretarial; data processing; domestic; medical/dental; professional; management; financial; insurance; restaurant/lounge; retailing; sales; technical; engineering; trades; and general employment.

Assuming the candidate has done his or her homework and has applied the principles and methods outlined in Chapter 2, it becomes a question of scanning the ads in the appropriate category and examining them closely.

You will notice that some of the ads are more descriptive than others. The following examples, taken from current classified sections, provide realistic samples of what you might find:

NEED WORK?
WE NEED 500 PEOPLE WHO CAN SPEAK SPANISH AND
ENGLISH. ALL SHIFTS. CALL _ _ _ _ _ _ _ _ _ _. AJAX TEM-
PORARY STAFFING.

PUBLIC RELATIONS
Immediate openings. Good benefits and training.
Up to $1500.00/mo. Advance to supervisor—12 weeks.
Women encouraged. Call _ _ _ _ _ _ _ _ _ _.
Atlantic Real Estate, Beach Office.

MARKETING RESEARCH MANAGER
Our company is a subsidiary of the Ajax Co., and a leading re-
searcher, marketer, and manufacturer of consumer skin care
products.
The individual will be responsible for the following areas:

- Analysis of secondary research, including sales audits.
- Planning and recommendations of survey research among
  consumers and medical professionals.
- Marketing science applications, including forecasting, sta-
  tistical analysis, and computer application.

The successful candidate will have a graduate degree, minimum 3 – 5
years related work experience with a consumer and/or skin products
manufacturer, and strong communication and participatory management
skills.
We are offering the candidate $50,000K + and excellent fringe benefits.
For confidential consideration, please send resume and salary history
to:
Personnel, Box KBW1520, Personal Products, Amherst, N.Y. 14440.

The first ad, for bilingual workers, is very brief and the candidate would be hard pressed to figure out much about the job from
the few bits of information offered. We do know that it involves an
employment agency and that they need 500 people with a bilingual
language capability. Beyond this, we know that it is shift work.
Anything else we might get out of the ad is pure speculation. Is it a
telemarketing position? Does it involve translating? Is it full-time or
part-time?

When dealing with an ad of this sort, about the only thing that you can do is make a list of prioritized questions before you call the company to make an interview appointment. It might include some of the following:

"What type of work is involved?"
"Is it full-time or part-time?"
"Is it temporary or permanent?"
"When do the various shifts start and end?"
"What company would I be working for?"
"What specific skills are you looking for?"
"Where is the company located?"
"Is it a salaried position or does it involve an hourly wage?"
"How much does it pay?"

This last question may seem to contradict advise presented elsewhere in the book since it is generally unwise to ask about money before a final selection interview takes place. On the other hand, since you have no idea of the wages involved, you must ask this question or risk wasting your time. In any case, asking any of the above questions only makes sense; otherwise, you cannot properly prepare for the interview, and you will place yourself in a very vulnerable position.

It is true that some companies, particularly employment agencies, will not divulge much information at this stage. There are various reasons for this, and some companies are quite adamant on this point; nevertheless, this should not stop you from trying.

The second sample ad, the one calling for "Public Relations," is a bit easier to decipher. Here we know that the employer is a real estate broker and the office is in the vicinity of the "Beach." We also learn that the position involves training, "good" benefits, and a monthly income of up to $1500. Finally, the ad tells us that advancement to supervisor is possible in 12 weeks and that women are encouraged to apply. Yet, in spite of the fact that this ad is more complete than the last, it still leaves more out than it includes.

For instance, "Public Relations" is a very broad term. Does the job involve public contact work? Is it a job soliciting appointments over the telephone? Will the candidate be expected to write copy? On another point, do you have to have a college degree to get the job? Exactly what are the qualifications? We also do not know if the position is salaried or hourly and what the starting wage is.

Then, there is the question of whether the "women encouraged" clause isn't really a directive to discourage men from applying. So, once again, it becomes a matter of making a list of appropriate questions to ask when calling for an appointment.

A word of caution is in order at this point, particularly in this situation. You cannot demand too much more information over the phone, particularly in the area of wages and benefits. They have told you enough in the ad for the time being. To demand additional information makes it sound as though this is all you care about. At the very least, you may seem pushy.

I recall that I once received a call from a candidate for a job as vice president of operations for a major medical supply company. Almost immediately he began to ask about wages and benefits.

"I'm calling about the ad you ran in the paper."

"Well," I answered, "the position is with a major . . . ." Before I could go any further, he interrupted.

"How much does it pay and what about the fringes?" he demanded.

"As it says in the ad, the position pays from $50,000 to $75,000 a year depending on experience and other qualifications. The benefit package is also variable," I answered.

"Yeah, but I'm not going to come to an interview unless you can be more specific," he said emphatically.

"I'm sorry," I said, "but I can't be more specific. Thank you for calling." I then hung up the telephone.

It might seem to the reader that I was being rude or somehow inappropriate in ending the conversation that way, but I had no further use for the caller. The ad in this case was sufficiently clear to indicate that the position was a very responsible one and a person who was so interested in wages and benefits couldn't be trusted to do the job. Presumably, he would spend most of his time thinking about his paycheck and vacations.

The last ad in question recruiting for a marketing research manager, is so complete there is no need to ask any questions in arranging for an interview appointment. It offers a brief but meaningful job description, tells you what basic qualifications are necessary, names and describes the company involved, and tells you what you can expect to be paid. Granted, it is not absolutely complete, but it does explain enough to allow the candidate to decide whether or not he or she is interested in proceeding any further.

Now, there are some ads that you should simply ignore. They are either very misleading or so vague that following up on them will waste your time and energy, or possibly cheat you. The following example is a case in point.

<u>WORK AT HOME</u>
$10-$15 an hour
no experience necessary
call: 343-2831

This ad actually tells you nothing about the job it promotes aside from the idea that you can work at home. Beyond this, it is essentially insulting. It presumes that you are so stupid or gullible that you will actually believe that without experience or a particular skill, you will make more per hour than many skilled craftsman or highly trained office personnel.

If you called the number in the ad you would probably discover that it is a telephone solicitation operation where the employee is expected to set up sales appointments for a home improvement company or possibly a vacuum cleaner dealer or some such thing. You are paid on the basis of how many actual appointments you make and whether or not the salesperson closes a sale with your prospect. While it might be possible to make "$10-$15 an hour," the prospects of doing so are so remote it isn't worth the bother. Moreover, you would probably have to use your own telephone, work at inconvenient hours, and put up with a lot of needless aggravation. I will admit that some people might actually enjoy such work or earn enough to make it worthwhile; but, they are the exception rather than the rule.

The obvious reason that this ad is so vague is that the company doing the recruiting knows about the drawbacks in this type of work. They also know that if they spell things out clearly, very few people will apply. So, by being incomplete, they are deliberately misleading.

Occasionally, you will see another ad that is very similar to the telephone solicitation ad. This one promises the same type of hourly wage but it calls for you to stuff envelopes in your home. Once again, you are soliciting, only this time it is through the mail. And, as frequently as not, you are expected to furnish your own stamps!

The basic rule of thumb is that if an ad is so vague you have no idea of what you would be applying for, don't bother with it.

TRADE PUBLICATIONS/JOURNALS

Most professions or trades have their own publications. Some of them feature classified ads for positions that range from high-level executives to entry-level training. Generally, though, these publications tend to offer higher paying jobs than you will find in the typical American daily newspaper.

One such monthly journal is published by the American Association of University Professors. It is titled, "The Chronicle of Higher Education." "The Chronicle" features a substantial number of ads for educational administrators, development specialists, professors, etc.

There are several strong advantages in turning to the trade or professional publications. First, the ads are job specific; that is, they tend to eliminate the generic and offer very specialized jobs calling for very specialized credentials. They also spell out the job and benefits in great detail and explain the background and experience that they want in an ideal candidate. In short, you know *exactly* what you are applying for and the qualifications they are looking for. Second, they are very selective in the ads that they take, and they usually screen the ads to make sure they are legitimate and related to the trade or profession. So you can trust the ads that they publish.

Unfortunately, trade and professional journals are seldom available at local newsstands, but the local public library may carry them. Also, most college or university libraries subscribe to a variety of journals.

Although the rules may vary from one location to another, most institutions of higher education will gladly allow nonstudents to use their library facilities if the individual registers at the main desk and has a legitimate reason for being there.

EMPLOYMENT AGENCIES

Basically, employment agencies can be grouped in two ways: those that specialize and those that don't.

The specialized agency may concentrate on engineers, or sales, or possibly clerical employees. It appears that more and more agencies are taking this approach because it is to their market advantage; that is, they can become known as the specialists in a particular area. The Kelly Services Co. (formerly known as Kelly Girls), for example, has been very successful for years by primarily placing female clerical personnel in specific types of jobs.

As a former owner of my own employment agency, I can personally attest to the advantage for the employee. First, specialized agencies tend to represent the higher-paying jobs. That is because employers with special needs (usually willing to pay more money to get what they want) turn to them first. Second, the placement personnel are often experts in a given area and they know where the jobs are. And third, many specialized agencies will actually train you to help make you more qualified.

The other side of the coin is that specialized agencies will not try to place you if you do not have the particular skill they are interested in. In fact, they may not even take your application. It is then that you will have to turn to the general agency.

General agencies are very willing to talk to just about anyone, no matter what their background happens to be. That is because the jobs they place are so varied that they never know when they are going to need a person with practically any type of skill or experience. However, since they really are not experts in any field, they frequently don't know if the candidate is really qualified, even if they try to test them. The net effect is that they frequently file your application away and then never call you.

On top of all this, these general agencies wind up with the lower paying jobs to place. Because their track record is often spotty, employers tend to shy away from them.

Another consideration for the job candidate is whether or not he or she has to pay the placement fee him or herself. Some agencies demand payment from the first week's paycheck. Others want a fee before they actually place you. Still others obtain their fee from the employer. No matter what the case is, be sure that you understand the financial situation before you get too involved.

In my experience, the most legitimate agencies charge the employer the fee rather than the job seeker. There are a number of reasons for this. For one thing, the agency should not receive anything until they actually get you a job. That, after all, is the reason that you used them in the first place. For another, if the job is important enough to the employer, he or she will gladly pay the relatively small fee to get the right person. If the employer isn't willing to invest the fee money, he or she is saying a lot about the position in question and how he or she intends to treat the person hired.

One last thing should be said about agencies. Most of them will do everything they can to place you in a job. It is in their own best interest. But that can also be a problem. Sometimes they are so eager to place you that they may send you to jobs that you are not really qualified for.

Once, I was sent to an interview as a structural engineer. I had background in this area and, from what I was told by the agency, I was more than qualified. When I got there, I was totally stunned and thoroughly embarrassed. My discomfort began almost immediately.

"Well, we're told that you have a lot of experience in thermal engineering," the interviewer said.

"Oh," I stumbled, ". . . . . . that's not really true."

"What do you mean?"

"As you can see from my resume, my . . . ."

"They didn't send along a resume," she said with an edge in her voice. "All I have is this."

What she showed me was a summary of my application and resume. It had been altered severely. I apologized for the misrepresentation and left. Since that unsettling experience, I have seen this sort of thing happen again and again. Underqualified applicants from agencies have turned up in my office repeatedly over the years and the situation seems to be getting worse.

Certainly, not every agency will deliberately falsify information about job candidates in order to place them. Still, it is a real problem and the reader should beware of the possibility.

In summary, employment agencies can be useful. But they have their limitations and should be used, in general, as a last resort.

PROFESSIONAL HEADHUNTERS

Unlike the run-of-the-mill employment agency, the typical professional headhunter company, or executive search firm, is extremely careful in guaranteeing the qualifications of its candidates.

The reason for this care is simple: they charge the employer enormous sums of money for their services and they can't afford to make mistakes. Their reputations would suffer and they would go out of business.

Because of this problem, most executive search firms are extremely selective in choosing the candidates that they decide to represent. In fact, registering with, or even finding one of these companies, can be very difficult. In some major cities they are listed in the yellow pages of the telephone directory. In most instances, however, you will find that they will contact you if they are interested in you. They will get your name from associates, professional mailing lists, or from competitors who know you and want you to work for them.

The Wall Street Journal is one of the few places that has regular listings from executive search firms. Apparently, these agencies believe that sufficient numbers of top rate executives read the paper so they are willing to expose themselves to public scrutiny.

If you have the good fortune to involve yourself with a headhunter agency, the probability of successful placement is very high. Consider yourself lucky.

NETWORKING

After all has been said and done, networking is the most effective way to get a job. Networking, quite simply, is using your professional (even your personal) contacts to find work. There are a number of ways to do this.

First, consider the social groups to which you belong. What church do you attend? What clubs do you belong to? With what informal groups do you socialize? All of these offer basic opportunities for the job seeker. If you let it be known that you are looking for a job, people may be able to direct you to an opening or even recommend you.

Second, consider your friends. Each person that you know, in turn, knows other people. When you start multiplying all of the people involved, the possibilities are surprising. Each of these individuals is a possible source for a job.

Third, nearly all professions have associations. These organizations are a tremendous source of information and opportunity for the job seeker. For instance, if you are a member of the local chapter of the American Society for Training and Development, you will be interacting with professionals in the field who will know where the jobs are. Also, if you interact with these people, they will get to know you and if they like you, they may hire you themselves or recommend you to their bosses.

A female executive that I know has found two excellent positions this way. Ten years ago, she had just graduated from college with a degree in communications, and was unemployed. Her only real previous experience was working as a waitress. Although she was not employed and had never worked in public relations, she joined the local professional association representing that field, and got to know a lot of people who apparently liked her. Within six months she was the public relations director of a local public service agency. When she left that job, she found another by networking through the same association.

If you are not a member of a professional organization, you can find one that might interest you by contacting the local Chamber of Commerce. If they can't help you, such information may be available in the public library. Even the library department of the local newspaper may be of help. Finally, you can try the library of a local college or university. As was indicated earlier, most institutions of higher education allow you to use their library resources in-house if you register at the circulation desk.

Networking may cost you some money, as most associations charge rather hefty annual dues. The process will often take a bit of time. Once you join, you will have to get to know people, and that can take months. The cost in time and money will be worth it.

4

The Interviewing Process

THE EMPLOYMENT INTERVIEW OCCURS IN STEPS OR STAGES, MUCH like a ball game. And, it can be diagrammed like one as well. This chapter breaks the process into component parts and describes the interaction accordingly.

THE PRELIMINARY POSITIONS

Before the interview actually begins, both parties are uncertain about the situation. The interviewer has no idea what you are like, and in most cases he or she is not really prepared for what is about to take place. Even armed with formal, prepared questions and a well-defined format, the interviewer is still in a difficult spot because *he or she desperately wants you to be the right person*. It may be that management is leaning on the supervisor to fill the post or that production conditions are forcing the department to hire an employee immediately. Or perhaps the interviewer is just sick and tired of seeing candidates. No matter what the reason, 99 percent of the time, the interviewer will do everything he or she can to give you the job, even if you are only marginally suited for the position. If the applicant will just cooperate, the interviewer will actually try to persuade a candidate to take the position.

The applicant usually wants the job or he or she would not be there in the first place. At the same time, the applicant has doubts and is generally uncertain about many factors. Is this a job for which he or she is really qualified? Is this a job that he or she will like? What about the pay and benefits? In addition to considering these questions, applicants will constantly try to please the interviewer in order to win the position.

So, the interviewer wants the candidate to be the right person for the job and to take it when the job is offered. The applicant wants the right job to be offered. In essence, both parties really want the same thing. But unfortunately, neither will admit this fact and, as a consequence, they engage in a complex game that rivals even the most advanced chess match.

THE OPENING MOVES

As a rule, the first opening move belongs to the employer. After all, the interviewer sets the time, date, location, and conditions for the interview and determines the general tone of the discussion. The interviewer also decides what questions to ask and what information to provide about the position or company. In this sense, the interviewer is immediately in control, or at the very least, has most of the elements on his or her side.

Most employers begin by trying to put the candidate at ease. Exactly why they do this is not clear. Perhaps it is because of some naive notion that this way the interviewer will get to see the "real" person. Or maybe it is the first step in trying to sell the job to the candidate. In any case, this informal approach begins with a greeting, a handshake, and quite often, an offer of a refreshment (see chapter 6).

Behind all of this seemingly friendly behavior, of course, is a mind-set that hopes this is the person for the job. Off-setting this, however, is a fundamental caution that says "I am not going to be fooled by this person. If this is not the right candidate, I will find out. I won't be tricked."

The opening for the employer is ambivalent, at best. On the one hand, the interviewer wants to impress the candidate and help him or her relax. On the other hand, the interviewer is suspicious and determined to cross-examine each applicant.

The opening for the candidate, of course, is much the same as the employee. The applicant, too, is generally uncomfortable because he or she probably wants the job but has no idea if it is *really* the right job. On top of this, applicants often are unsure about what to say and sometimes are confused about how to act. So the candidate usually tries to play it safe by acting casual and friendly and responding with short answers to the initial greeting.

At this point, of course, neither party is being perfectly honest. It is similar to the greeting of two prize fighters in the center of the ring. Although the rules dictate that they shake hands and behave like gentlemen, what they both want is to win and they are prepared to beat each other to a pulp to do it. In the same way, the employer and the candidate are playing out similar roles. They might smile and shake hands and sound like two friends, but the reality is quite different. At this stage, they are combatants who are feeling each other out. Each side is determined to win the round and eventually the battle, even if it means discomfort.

There are those who claim that the typical interview is filled with good will and deep regard for the other party, and that the outward appearance of friendliness at the beginning is genuine. But such a view presumes that the main purpose of the interaction is social; the interviewer and the interviewee have little at stake in the outcome; and each has nothing to hide. To assume that the above is true is naive, wishful thinking that ignores reality.

The opening is a test. Both parties gently fence with one another, size each other up, and make last-minute battle plans. Appearances aside, it is the quiet before the interviewing storm.

Incidentally, the typical opening does not last more than five minutes or so, but it can continue for much longer if the employer wishes or allows this to happen. It is usually to the advantage of the candidate to extend the opening of course, because doing so will limit the time spent dealing with harder, much more demanding questions.

I once watched a woman, being interviewed for a position as a university professor, maneuver herself into a situation like this that lasted nearly an hour. I happened to be there because I was the chairperson who brought her to the dean to be interviewed. The moment we walked into his office the dean began a meaningless discussion about some trivial matter that had nothing to do with why we were there. The candidate picked up on it and continued to amplify her thoughts on the subject for the next fifty minutes. I sat there astonished because the dean (a person I regarded as bright and observant) did not seem to notice what the candidate was doing. But for reasons of her own, she kept it up until we had nearly run out of time. As it turned out, the dean was only able to ask her a few basic questions, which produced only a minumum of information. Yet, when I spoke to him about the candidate the next day, he seemed perfectly sure that she was the right person for the job. He even commented that he "enjoyed the interview" and that I should hire her.

THE BODY

After pleasantries have been exchanged, the important part of the interview begins. That is not to say that the opening is unimportant; far from it. The opening is filled with information and it is where significant first impressions will be formed. But that information and those first impressions are put to the test in the body of the interview where data leads to insight, and insight leads to action.

The body of the employment interview begins the moment the interviewer asks the first question about the individual's background or begins to describe the position. In either case, it is the signal that the serious business of interview is commencing and that the friendly chitchat is over. In most interviews this change is quite obvious and is frequently more abrupt than one would expect. The employer immediately assumes a more resolute tone. With a lowered voice and fewer smiles, the interviewer's body becomes more rigid. The candidate also becomes stiff and is suddenly more serious. In short, both parties intuitively recognize that the game has begun.

Because the employer begins the interview, he or she is initially in charge. But that advantage may be short lived unless the interviewer is careful. In order to get all of the information needed, the interviewer must be careful not to inadvertently turn control of the interview over to the candidate. This can and often does happen in the first few minutes, and it usually occurs because the interviewer asks broad, spontaneous questions that allow the applicant to take the conversation in any direction (see chapter 6).

The most effective interviews, from an employer perspective, are deductive or funnel shaped. That is, they start with general questions that are followed up with more specific targeted questions, called *probes*, that gain the employer needed additional information. But, such carefully structured employment interviews are rare. The interview that you can expect to take part in will be much more random. In fact, some of the questions will probably not seem to make much sense. (While being interviewed for a job, I was once asked by the chief engineer of a corporation if I liked classical music.)

But even if the questions seem directionless, there is a thought and intention behind them. It has been my experience that practically no one ever asks an employment interview question without some clear motive. And, if the interviewer is competent, he or she will seek as much factual material as possible from the applicant. Unfortunately for most companies, but fortunately for you, the average interviewer seems to get confused on this point; that is, an interviewer sometimes treats inferences and opinions as facts. For example, the question, "Have you ever been fired from a job?" asks for a factual response. If the candidate answers that he or she always likes to leave jobs voluntarily, the inference is that the candidate has never been fired. And if the applicant says that he or she thinks being fired from a job is a disgrace, that is simply offering an opinion. Yet, most interviewers will accept either answer as fact. The point is that the interviewer has satisfied a motive.

The candidate also has motives, of course, and they are seldom the same as the employer's. If the employer wants information of one sort or another, the candidate's motive is to create a favorable impression. As a rule, the applicant will try to second-guess the interviewer. Occasionally, the individual will even control the direction of the questioning by offering information that suggests other questions to the employer. Second-guessing of any sort, of course, is a dangerous game to play. Although some interviewers are more transparent than others, there is no way that you can ever be sure that you are on the right track and that you really know what is going on in the interviewer's mind. Nevertheless, it is a natural response and a common phenomenon in the give and take of the employment interview.

So, the interview progresses with the interviewer probing and the applicant second-guessing until the time is up or the employer runs out of questions.

THE CONCLUSION

The standard end to the employment interview is for the interviewer to indicate that he has no further questions. Sometimes the interviewer will ask the candidate if he or she has any questions.

But that statement is often nothing more than a polite way to finish the interview. Some interviewers do not really want questions and are surprised when they are posed. I can speak from direct experience. Everytime I have used that approach I have been startled, even annoyed, if the candidate takes me up on my question. For one thing, it implies that I have not been complete or clear in providing important information. Also, it prolongs the interview past a point that satisfies me.

I can also testify from experience that nine out of ten candidates have no questions. I am not sure why that is the case but the vast majority of applicants seem content to just say goodbye. Maybe they are so worn out that the only thing they want is to be out of the room. Or perhaps it is a question of not being able to think of anything important at the time. Whatever it is, the typical candidate will thank the interviewer and depart.

Occasionally, the interviewer will end the interview with a statement indicating that he or she will contact the candidate within a certain timeframe. More often, however, the interviewer will just indicate that he will "be in touch" with the candidate when the employer arrives at a decision. This, of course, is of little comfort to the candidate. But it is a convenient way to leave the prospective employee some room for hope while at the same time it does not commit the employer to any position.

THE AFTERMATH OF THE INTERVIEW

From an informational point of view, the net result of all of this effort is usually less than perfect. As often as not, the employer comes away with an inaccurate picture of the prospect, and the candidate leaves somewhat confused and wondering how well he or she did.

From a psychological perspective, the typical employment interview can be exhausting for both parties. The game of cat and mouse strains even the most expert participants as they seek or withhold information, trade strategies and tactics, and struggle for control. Even a superficial look at nearly any employment interview will demonstrate that it has taken a considerable toll.

It is normal for the candidate to feel the greatest impact because he or she has been under cross examination. An overall letdown feeling is common, with the applicant wishing he or she had or had not done this or that. But the interviewer frequently feels the effect of the pressure as well because he or she has had to anticipate answers, make up spur-of-the-moment probes, and make sense out of a situation that is filled with confusion.

Obviously, some interviews do not follow a pattern and some interviews result in a much clearer picture than is indicated here. They are the exception rather than the rule.

You can minimize the negative impact of an employment interview on yourself as a candidate if you follow the advice in the remaining chapters. But no matter how well prepared you are, the employment interview will generally seem a confusing, tiring experience that seems best from a distance.

5

What You Can Expect When You Get There

MOST PEOPLE TEND TO BELIEVE THAT THE TYPICAL EMPLOYMENT interviewer is highly skilled and reasonably well trained in the interviewing process; however, as has been suggested in other chapters, the facts do not support this.

LACK OF INTERVIEWER EXPERTISE

As a rule, the person who will interview you for a job will not have *any* training in this process. The vast majority of them are "retreads" from some other area of experience or expertise. It is not at all uncommon for a human resource or personnel director to come to the job with a management or legal background. Such backgrounds may be useful in some aspects of human resources, but they do little to prepare a person for the unique conditions of hiring someone. Still, even if they are trained in personnel management, it is doubtful that the individual has been exposed to any sort of formal education in employment interviewing. (If he or she has, he or she probably has learned a lot of textbook nonsense.) For example, I recently conducted a thorough investigation of business colleges in search of courses in interviewing at the undergraduate or even the graduate level. I found that virtually none were offered anywhere. While communication departments at major universities will sometimes include interviewing as part of other courses, the material is frequently very general and essentially useless as background for hiring.

Now, it is true that numerous management development organizations offer workshops on so-called effective employment interviewing. But in my direct experience, they are not very well attended. Beyond that, the material is generally weak and frequently impractical because it is based on old notions and little meaningful research. Take, for example, that most employment interviewing seminars still stress open-ended questions and "gut" reactions to personalities. Because of this, they don't really help much and the people who attend them leave with the feeling that they are now experts in this area. Of course, they are not. Nevertheless, the fact that most interviewers don't know what they are doing is a significant advantage to you when you show up to be interviewed for a job.

The first thing you can expect is that the individual will be poorly prepared to interview you even though he or she doesn't know it.

THE TYPICAL EMPLOYMENT INTERVIEW FORMAT

Given that most organizations and their representatives are not very sophisticated when it comes to selecting employees, it is simply enough to predict what you can expect to experience.

The Opening

Normally, you will be greeted with meaningless references to the weather or a sporting event or some such thing. The interviewer has probably been told (one way or another) that it is a good idea to begin this way because it allegedly "puts the candidate at ease." There is very little evidence to indicate that this actually will happen, but it doesn't matter. What should concern you is that it gives you a chance to show off the positive aspects of your personality and gain the upper hand from the outset.

Later we will explain exactly how to handle this type of opening. For now, it is enough to know that this is what you can expect nine times out of ten.

If the employer does begin with an opening of this sort, it is possible that he or she will follow up by describing his or her organization and/or the job itself. In either case, if you listen carefully, the interviewer may give you valuable information about the overall philosophy of the business and even what is expected in an employee.

Take, for example, a client of mine (an extremely well-educated and successful businessman, and president of his own company), who asked me to sit in on a series of interviews he was conducting in his search for an executive vice-president for his firm. He was hoping that I could give him some pointers to improve his interviewing skill.

When the candidate first sat down, the president immediately began to describe his company to the prospective employee.

"You see," he began, "this company is based on a very simple philosophy. We believe that no one person can run a business of this sort without relying on others to help. In a word, it's a question of teamwork. We are successful because we work together, because we truly trust and respect one another. So the person we hire as executive vice-president has to be a team player." He then began to describe the specifics of the job. When he finished, he said, "Now, tell me why we should hire you as executive vice-president instead of 15 other people? What special quality do you think you bring to us?"

Not surprisingly, the man being interviewed eventually ended his long-winded response by saying, ". . . and I guess because I'm a team player. If you contact anybody I've ever worked with, they will confirm my willingness to work with others toward a common goal. From what you've said, teamwork seems to be a foundation of this company, so I'd fit right in."

When the interview was over, my client said to me that he didn't think he had to look at anyone else; that he had found his man. Naturally, I was astonished and I asked him what he meant?

"This guy is a natural. He's got the credentials. Besides that, he's a team player and you know how important that is to me."

"How do you know he's a team player," I insisted.

"Well, he said so. In fact, he made a strong point about his willingness to work with others."

At this juncture, I explained why the gentleman had felt compelled to claim to be a team player and that he had been told how to respond. It is important to bear in mind that the interviewer in this case should have been aware of the mistake he had made. But he did not until it was pointed out to him.

Not every interviewer will be this obvious in giving you infor-mation. But if you listen carefully, he or she will almost always give you clues regarding what he or she is looking for. Even if he doesn't do this immediately (if he moves directly into the questions he intends to ask), you can tactfully interrupt him by turning an answer into a question. That is, you can simply ask the interviewer what he is looking for in a candidate.

The Questions

Once the employer has opened the interview, you can be reason-ably certain he or she will then turn to those open-ended questions I referred to earlier. Such questions ask for your opinion, your thoughts, and seldom demand any real proof or substantive evi-dence. So you can answer any way you want. The list of probable questions presented in chapter 6 is very typical of those used in most organizations.

The questions ramble with little sequence and frequently ask for inane and useless information. For instance, once when I was applying for a summertime job as a janitor in a hospital, I was asked if I had any hobbies. When I answered that "I enjoy painting impressionistic city-scapes," the personnel director stared at me for what seemed like a full minute and then mumbled, "I see. Well, that's nice I guess." Just why he wanted to know about my hob-bies, or what they told him about my ability to do the job, I can't possibly imagine. Another time, I was asked by an employer if I had bad habits. Naturally, I told him no and that seemed to satisfy him.

Occasionally, a more sophisticated approach may be taken to the interview process. This occurs when the organization in ques-tion uses standardized, closed-ended questions. These types of questions demand a specific answer such as yes or no, an exact number, or even the in-depth explanation of a technical process.

The following list contains examples of closed-ended ques-tions:

- Have you ever been fired from a job? Yes or no?
- Do you know how to boot up the Apple Writer II on an Apple IIE computer? Yes or no? Explain.
- Would you ever refuse to do what your boss says? Yes or no? Explain.

- Do you feel an engineer should routinely work overtime? Yes or no? Explain.

Fortunately, for those seeking employment, closed-ended questions are the exception, not the rule. So there is little reason to expect them.

SINGLE INTERVIEW SITUATION

In this situation, you have your best chance of landing the position for which you are applying. This is also the most common interviewing experience.

Generally, the interview will take place in the office occupied by the employer. The employer is the only one you can expect to see and is the person who will do the actual hiring.

The interviewer will have your resume or completed application in hand, and if he doesn't have questions prepared in advance he will simply draw them from the information that you have given him. In this case, he is limited by the data in front of him; data supplied and controlled by you. If you write that you once studied aviation mechanics, he might ask you about that. If you don't, he can hardly ask you about it.

In addition, if he or she is like most interviewers, what you look and sound like will be more important than the specific content of your answers. So all you have to do is impress one person under conditions favorable to you.

Single interview situations are most common in small organizations where the employer does not have a human resource person, but there are exceptions. For instance, the personnel director in a large corporation might have authority to hire the administrative assistant without having to have him or her to talk to the head of the accounting department.

Whoever conducts it, a single interview situation will be the standard. It will also offer you your best opportunity to land the job.

ROUND ROBIN INTERVIEW

The round robin interview is conducted by some companies for several reasons: It generates a number of impressions of a given candidate, implying that this type of interview presents a more accurate understanding of the candidates ability to do the job; and, it distributes responsibility in case the wrong person is hired.

The round robin interview is particularly popular when large corporations hire management personnel. Since these employees must interact with a variety of people, and since they must often understand a wide range of processes and systems, it is thought that this type of questioning will give the most complete picture of the individual. (In actual fact, there is no reason to believe that this is true.)

Sometimes the round robin will consist of an initial screening interview at the human resource or personnel department level, followed by a final selection interview conducted by the functional department head. In this situation, it is very important to make a good initial impression on the first interviewer because: a) you won't get a chance to see the boss if this person isn't positively impressed; b) he or she will invariably provide a picture of you that will affect the department head's vision of your ability to fit in and do the job.

Less frequently, the round robin is conducted by a comparatively large number of people of various backgrounds. You are taken from one office to another and asked different questions from a wide variety of perspectives. Because each person is interested in a different aspect of your ability to do the job, the pictures that emerge of you can differ significantly from person to person; this process can pose real accuracy problems.

This system presupposes that every person that interviews you is interested in helping to fill the job. A few years ago, a major chemical company contacted me to do some advanced management training. Because it involved a number of important middle managers from around the nation, I was asked to come to the headquarters for interviews with top management to see if I was the "right man" to do the job. When I arrived, the corporate human resources director asked me some halting questions over coffee. When it became clear that he was thoroughly unprepared to talk to me, I recall saying, "Why don't I save us both a lot of time and tell you who I am, what I am prepared to do for your company, and then you can ask me anything else that I don't cover?" He was delighted to be relieved of the responsibility of coming up with meaningful questions and when I finished he stood up and said, "Sounds good to me. Why don't we see the President?" We walked down the hall to the President's office and his secretary announced us.

"Mr. Hendricks is here with Dr. Hammond," she said over the intercom.

"With whom?" asked the President.

"Dr. Hammond," she replied.

"I don't understand," he responded.

"It's about the management training, I believe," she continued.

"Oh . . . well, send them in," he said with resignation.

The truth was, of course, that he didn't really know what was going on, and even when he found out it was obviously a low priority for him. When he talked to me, I took the lead as I had with the human resources director. I saw four other people that morning and not one of them seemed to know or care why I was there. I got the contract for the training and everything worked out well, but not because they had fulfilled their responsibility!

In a real sense, the round robin interview operates to your benefit. For one thing, the questions are practically always open-ended allowing you to control things. For another, it permits you to make a strong impression on the greatest number of people. One person may or may not hire you, even if he or she thinks you are capable of doing the job. But five people, in nearly complete agreement about your ability, will act more decisively to hire you.

THE GROUP INTERVIEW

The rarest interview situation is the group interview. It is also the most threatening for most job applicants because they feel overwhelmed by sheer numbers.

The rationale for group interviews rests on the basic assumptions that: when an entire group interviews the applicant at the same time, the individuals tend to get the same general impression and can more easily reach consensus; and the pressure exerted by a group will bring out the so-called real person.

While there is little doubt that pressure can help generate more genuine responses from the interviewee, it is certainly not an automatic fact of life. Beyond that, the first contention regarding consensus is not supportable. As any psychologist will tell you, everyone sees something different in a common experience or event.

The great problem with group interviews, then, is not the pressure (though that is the feeling when you are under fire).

Rather, it is the fact that people seldom agree on a candidate's credentials and most of the group will simply give in to the most aggressive or powerful person. And if you didn't make a particularly strong positive impression on that one individual, you will not get the job.

The group interview really isn't a very effective device for either party in the recruitment process. It makes hiring decisions more difficult for the organization while it distorts the candidate's behavior and creates a confusing and nerve-racking situation for him or her. Still, there are organizations that continue to use group interviews. Happily for the candidate (and the organization), they are few and far between.

SCREENING DEVICES

Occasionally, you can expect to be confronted with screening devices. Many large organizations are turning to them early in the first stages of the process, in an effort to qualify candidates once it seems certain that the person meets the basic requirements to do the job. Then it becomes a question of sorting out the wheat from the chaff. That is, somehow deciding that a person possesses the *exact* qualifications to do the job well.

For the most part, these mechanisms are standardized tests that practically anybody can purchase from research-oriented publishers. Most of these exams have been validated (tested and confirmed for accuracy) and the employer picks out a variable or set of variables that he or she wants to test and buys the proper device to measure what he or she is looking for.

The problem with these tests is that they are usually so generic that they don't really do the employer much good. As scientific as they seem, they are not specific to the job and, at best, they either indicate very general tendencies, or else they plot a very narrow picture of one or two traits or abilities.

For the candidate, it invariably becomes a no-win situation. No matter how you try to second-guess the test, it is almost impossible to figure out how to respond. And even if you do figure out the "right" answers, the test may come back to haunt you later. For instance, if you score high on preferring to work alone as a technician, the test results may get you hired but they may prevent you from being promoted into a high person-contact management job in the future.

A variation on the screening test is the polygraph or lie detector. While the accuracy of this test has been in question for years, many employers still rely heavily on it, especially in the retail business where employees handle money and have easy access to tempting stock. There are those who claim they know how to "beat" these tests, but for the most part they are also very difficult to second-guess.

While such screening devices as generic psychological tests, aptitude tests, tendency tests, and polygraph examinations are used today on a selective basis, they are still the exception and don't pose a significant problem for most people seeking jobs.

THE END OF THE INTERVIEW

All of us would like to know whether or not we landed the job immediately after the interview. But that is seldom the case. Most organizations want to consider a number of people for a job rather than jumping at the first attractive applicant. Also, they may want to factor in the screening test before making a decision. Finally, they may not want to give you the bad news if it comes to that, or they may be prohibited from telling you because of regulations.

The net effect of all this is that you normally leave the interview with a feeling of uncertainty. But that does not always have to be true, if you know the signs to look for. As often as not, if you have made a strong favorable or unfavorable impression, the interviewer will indicate this fact. In the next chapter we will examine this notion and similar considerations.

6

How to Respond to the Interviewer

STUDIES IN THE FIELD OF COMMUNICATION AND PSYCHOLOGY indicate that most first impressions are formed in as little as five seconds, and that they are reasonably constant or unchanging. Therefore, the first few seconds of initial contact may be the most important of all. That being the case, it is essential that you completely understand the dynamics of the situation. As the old saying goes, "You never get a second chance to make a first impression."

THE INITIAL CONTACT

I will presume that you have followed suggestions in chapter 2 and have:

- created a positive resume (that got you the interview).
- dressed in conservative, clean business clothes.
- groomed yourself appropriately, making sure your hair is trimmed and/or neat and that your nails are clean.

However, there is much more to first impressions than clothes and good grooming. There is the question of how you behave.

Responding to the Greeting

As is indicated in chapter 3, most openings or greetings are informal and nondirective. The interviewer is typically uncertain of what to do at this point, beyond trying to put the applicant at ease. Therefore, this may be the point at which the employer is most vulnerable. Assuming this is the case, the candidate has enormous potential for manipulation and control; but, it is an advantage that is very fragile and very temporary. The question becomes one of careful preparation and demonstrated confidence.

The standard greeting begins with efforts at congeniality. Accordingly, the applicant should be equally friendly and outgoing. The key here is "equally." You should measure your behavior against that of the interviewer. If he or she says, "It is a beautiful day (referring to the weather)," you should agree with equal enthusiasm. By the same token, if he or she says, "Isn't it a miserable and rainy day," you should empathically agree. Anything short of complete agreement throws the greeting back at the interviewer and makes the person feel foolish or angry.

Perhaps a more specific example will be helpful. At one point, I was being recruited for a position with an Ivy League university. The dean of the college of business called me in for an interview. He started out by condemning higher administration officials for limiting my travel expenses and apologized for their behavior. In an effort to put him at ease, I told him that the university had been most generous and that I was perfectly happy with the arrangements. His response, rather than being appreciative of my understanding, was obvious and frozen anger. I was eventually hired for the position, but shortly after the interview the dean told a colleague of mine that, although I was going to be hired, he was concerned about my "attitude problem." So, it becomes a question of agreeing rather than arguing, even if your argument is designed to make someone feel better.

You should also scan the interviewer's office for clues regarding his or her personal life. Are there family pictures on the desk? Is there a bowling trophy on the shelf? Is there a Rotary Club plaque on the wall? All of these signs offer you opportunities to gain rapport with the interviewer. You can compliment the family, indicate your interest in bowling, or demonstrate your connection with or general support for the Rotary Club. However, you should proceed carefully along these lines.

Once when I was trying to sell a potential client on a consulting contract, I got into considerable difficulty because I assumed too much. The general manager of the plant had pictures of sailboats all over the walls of his office. Since I sail, I thought this would be a perfect opportunity to gain favor with him through a common interest.

"I see you are a sailboat enthusiast. I've been sailing for three years and I love it!" I exclaimed with a smile.

"Oh," he said. "The pictures. Frankly those were my wife's idea. I despise sailboats. As far as I'm concerned," he continued, "sailboats are a menace to navigation."

He made a few other disparaging remarks about sailing and then he dropped the subject. Naturally, I felt like a fool and my efforts almost cost me the contract. Again, making an effort to relate to the interviewer based on the items you see in the office is generally a good idea, but proceed with caution.

On another but related point, it is very common for the interviewer to offer you coffee or a hard or soft drink in the name of breaking the ice and being congenial. On balance, it is generally best to refuse the refreshment unless the issue is pressed and he or she insists. In that case, you should accept the drink in the spirit of agreement but barely touch it.

The reasoning behind the first suggestion is quite simple. Under high pressure, it is not uncommon to spill your drink. Nothing will eliminate you as a candidate quicker than ruining the interviewer's desk top, papers, or rug. It demonstrates your clumsiness or your inability to deal with tension or pressure. But even if you don't spill the drink, it is often a problem to find a place to put it down. The interviewer's desk is no answer; it is his or her territory and to place the glass or cup on the desk (with or without permission), is a violation of someone's personal space even if neither of you consciously recognize it.

As I said, if the interviewer insists on you having something to drink, put it in the most neutral spot you can find and forget it until you get up to leave. If it is alcohol, drinking it could destroy that fine edge between complete control and loss of control. Even if the drink is nonalcoholic, it could prove very difficult to handle as you try to gesture or look at printed material handed to you.

Acting Right

Your body language, the way you move your body, communicates a great deal to other people. This is almost exclusively a subconscious response and most people don't know that they are sending or receiving messages sent through this medium. Author Julius Fast, with his book *Body Language* (published in 1970), was among the first to popularize the well-researched notion that how you act may frequently be more important than what you actually say.

Neutral body language is having your hands at your side, your back straight, your head up and parallel to the ground, and your feet side by side and about eight to 10 inches apart. Everytime you move from this neutral position, you say something to other people.

In an interview situation, everything you do is magnified in importance including your actions. It is imperative, therefore, that you observe the following:

1. Walk into the room confidently, with your head up and your hands at your side. Be sure to keep your hands out of your pockets. Apparently, when your hands are in your pockets, people will tend to distrust you.

2. Smile momentarily but don't overdo it. Studies show that if you smile too long or too much, people will think that you are a friendly, but empty-headed fool.

3. Look the interviewer in the eyes when you are talking to him or her. There is substantial proof in hard research that good eye contact increases feelings of trust. Don't stare, but don't look down at the floor or out a window all the time, either.

4. Shake hands with your arm stretched out toward the other person. With your thumb straight up, slide your hand into the other person's, squeezing his hand firmly but briefly. Avoid the weakness of an arm held closely to the body with the elbow pressed against the side. This indicates timidity and lack of confidence. On the other hand, you should also avoid the macho tendency to crush the other person's hand.

5. Sit down with your legs uncrossed, your head up, and your arms in your lap or resting on the side of the chair. Don't cross your arms; it reportedly demonstrates defensiveness and holding back.

By now you may be saying to yourself, "This guy has to be kidding. It would be unnatural to act this way." Well, there is nothing natural about the interview situation, so you can hardly be expected to "act natural." Instead, you must be *controlled*. There is an old saying that proclaims, "Those in control of themselves, control events." By the same token, those who are out of control (show nervous reactions), tend to be controlled by others. Perhaps the following story will illustrate my point.

I was the president of a faculty association at a small college in New York State. An executive director of a large public school teachers' credit union had come to me with a proposal to allow our members to join his group. It was tempting to join because we were too small to have our own credit union and his organization offered many significant benefits. Still, I was uncertain about some of the specifics of his financial package so I asked him to present his pitch to our certified public accountant. I sat in on the presentation.

At the beginning, the executive director of the credit union was exuding confidence. He gestured freely, and when he wasn't waving his hands in the air, his body was in a neutral position. Suddenly, the C.P.A. asked a difficult question. In less than a second, the executive director stopped waving and crossed his arms over his chest. Another tough question followed. He crossed his legs as well and turned sideways in his chair with his shoulders pointing at his interrogator. Finally, when he was hit with a third probing question, he dropped his head and stared into his lap. He was obviously in a highly defensive posture and probably holding back information. After the interview, it was easy enough to predict that the C.P.A. would tell me not to join the credit union. The financial expert based his suggestion primarily on what the man said with words. I came to the same conclusion from what the man said with his body.

If you are saying to yourself, this is too much like witchcraft, that it sounds ridiculous, I don't blame you. At one point I would have been inclined to take the same position on body language. However, it may be comforting to know that the research in this area is very convincing.

But even if you are not convinced, you have little to lose and a great deal to gain by paying some attention to your body language. Most people will freely admit that they think that behavior reflects attitude. If that is the case, then you want to be cautious, if for no other reason than that you want to make the most favorable impression that you can. Many people fail to land the job they want because they were too nonverbally aggressive or passive without realizing it. Or perhaps it was smiling too much or shaking hands too loosely.

I recall presenting a candidate to a client who never got to first base because he almost crushed my client's hand. The president of the company was so angry he was almost beyond talking. The candidate was very qualified but he lost out because he apparently thought that it was important to be macho.

So, what it comes down to is that you must look and act properly from the moment you first enter the interviewer's territory. Anything short of that may automatically disqualify you no matter what other skills or qualifications you bring with you.

THE INTERVIEW

Most interviews begin and end with questions of one sort or another, so we will begin our consideration of this aspect with some typical examples of what you can expect to encounter.

The Open-Ended Questions

You will remember that open-ended questions are those that call for broad, subjective answers based on your opinion. The following is a list of the 25 most frequently asked open-ended questions and recommended generic answers to them.

1. Question: What qualifications do you possess that will help you in this job?
   Answer: Well, aside from the skills that you know about from my resume (or application), I guess it's my interest in being an integral part of the winning effort; one that makes a difference in the scheme of things. And I'm more than willing to give 150 percent if that's what it takes.

2. Question: How do you feel about travelling?
   Answer: If travelling is required to do the job, then that is what I would expect to do. I think that travelling can be exciting or boring depending on your attitude. I'm not saying that I would want to travel during my entire history with the company, but I do think that travelling for this company could be an exciting challenge.

3. Question: Why did you decide to become a _ _ _ _ _ _ _ _ _ _

(business, engineering, art, english, etc.) major in (college, school, etc.)?

Answer: I have always been fascinated by the field of _ _ _ _ _
_ _ _ _ _ (business, engineering, etc.) because of the opportunities it offers to anyone who looks for them. I suppose some people fall into their majors in school almost by accident, but my choice was deliberate. It's a question of admiring a profession and doing what it takes to join it.

4. Question: If you had your education to do all over again, what would you change?

   Answer: Not very much except maybe to gain more course experience in my field. I received a first rate education in _ _ _ _ _ _ _ _ _ _ (field) at _ _ _ _ _ _ _ _ _ _ (school, college, etc.) but it is my opinion that you can never be too well prepared if you want to work for a company like _ _ _ _.

5. Question: What do you know about our company?

   Answer: Not as much as I'd like to. I read your _ _ _ _ _ _ _ _ _
   _ (annual report, company newsletter, advertising material, brochure, newspaper story) and I was very impressed by _ _ _ _ _ _ _ _ _ _ (the range of your product line, market share, technology, enormous growth, sales last year, commitment to quality, financial position, interest in the environment, etc.). But I do have one question, if you don't mind. What will be the major thrust of your company in the next five years in terms of _ _ _ _ _ _ _ _ _ _ (market share, product line, diversification, growth, organizational development, etc.)?

6. Question: Why did you leave your last job?

   Answer: (If you left voluntarily.) It was a very deliberate choice because my job became too easy. It's not that it was too routine. It just wasn't as challenging as it once had been. I never stopped liking my work, and I had excellent support from my superiors. They did everything that they could to convince me to stay but I need to feel that I'm really contributing to my employer's success. And I think the position that you are trying to fill will provide me with that opportunity and the challenge it represents.

   Answer: (If you were fired or forced to resign.) I think there are times when the employer and employee have to come to grips with the reality of a situation that doesn't completely benefit either one. When that occurs, I think that mutual respect and common courtesy should prevail. In my case, an analysis of the situation convinced my employer and me that I had done everything that I could for the company and that it was time to leave. I am grateful for the opportunity that _ _ _ _ _ _ _ _ _ (company name) gave me and I have nothing but respect for _ _ _ _ _ _ _ _ _ _ (company name) as a _ _ _ _ _ _ _ _ _ _ (manufacturer, social service agency, distributor, educational institution, etc.).

7. Question: What are your personal plans and ambitions?
   Answer: For the immediate future, they center on finding a position like the one that I'm applying for here. In a real sense, I'm not sure that anyone can really separate their personal and professional aspirations. For the long term future, I think that largely depends on my relationship with my next employer. Again, I'm not sure that personal and professional plans can ever be really separated.

8. Question: How do you spend your spare time?
   Answer: Well, I'm sure you will agree that most hobbies are extensions of what a person chooses to do for a living. In my case, I'm a _ _ _ _ _ _ _ _ _ (name of your profession) and _ _ _ _ _ _ _ _ _ (hobby or outside interest) improves my _ _ _ _ _ _ _ _ _ _ _ _ _ _ (concentration, patience, interpersonal relations, analytic ability, sense of timing, ability to plan, ability to deal with pressure, willingness to let go, sense of proportion, willingness to make decisions, etc.).

9. Question: Describe the kind of boss for whom you would like to work.
   Answer: What I'd want in a boss is honesty and fairness. I'm a flexible person when it comes to working with different sorts of people so I'm not sure anything else would really matter to me. As long as he or she is honest and fair I'm sure I could get along with him or her.

10. Question: What are your professional goals as far as this company is concerned?
    Answer: Frankly, I think that is more or less up to the company itself. Naturally, I would like to develop myself as much as possible, but I'd have faith in my superiors to determine where I'd fit in best.

11. Question: How do you personally measure success?
    Answer: I would say that a person is successful when he or she accomplishes what he or she sets up to do. In my professional life I measure success in terms of productivity. It isn't always a question of finishing what you set out to do. It must be done efficiently, and at the lowest possible cost in order to guarantee the well-being of the organization.

12. Question: Why do you want to work for this company?
    Answer: Mostly because of your _____ (reputation, quality services or products, growth pattern, conservative or progressive approach, concern for people, team approach, track record on social issues, etc.). When I first considered applying for this position, I did a lot of research to find out as much as I could about _____ (company name). I liked what I found out and that's why I'm here.

13. Question: What extra-curricular activities did you take part in at school?
    Answer: I was most active in _____ (sports, honor society, club, etc.). I found that getting involved in that activity helped to develop my _____ (ability to concentrate, spirit of teamwork, concern for details, interest in careful planning, positive outlook, etc.).
                          or
    Answer: I didn't have much time for extra-curricular acitivites because of _____ (working, my course load, personal commitments, etc.). Still, I think that situation was more positive than anything else because it helped to develop my ability to _____ (deal with pressure, concentrate, handle difficult people, deal with procrastination, plan things out, etc.).

14. Question: What do you really want to do in life?
    Answer: As far as I am concerned, the only way I can answer that is to say that I want to be the best _____ (mechanic, engineer, nurse, manager, accountant, sales person, etc.) that I can possibly be. It doesn't really matter to me where I end up in the organization as long as I know deep inside that I am making a real contribution.

15. Question: What do you expect to be earning five years from now?
    Answer: I want to be earning what my employer thinks I am worth. To put it another way, I wouldn't join an organization unless I trusted their judgement concerning my value to them. In any case, money isn't as important as the satisfaction of doing a good job.

16. Question: Which is more important to you; money or the type of job you get?
    Answer: Money is important, of course, but not as important as the feeling of accomplishment when you are achieving results in a job that makes a significant difference. So, I would say that the type of job is more important than money, because money is just part of the end result of doing a significant job well.

17. Question: What are your greatest strengths and weaknesses?
    Answer: I believe that my greatest strength is my willingness to put out 110% to get the job done. If that means long hours and hard work, I can accept that fact. On the other hand, I believe my greatest weakness is that I tend to work too hard at times, even at my own expense.

18. Question: How would you describe yourself?
    Answer: As a worker, I would describe myself as a person who is _ _ _ _ _ _ _ _ _ _ (thorough, hard working, ethical, agressive, self-starting, determined, a problem-solver, a team player, a company person, etc.). From what you have told me about the position, I think that my tendancy to be _ _ _ _ _ _ _ _ _ (thorough, hard working, etc.) would be a definite asset to _ _ _ _ _ _ _ _ _ (name of company).

19. Question: What motivates you?
    Answer: The feeling that what I am doing is important. The more I'm challenged, the better I like it. Of course, it's not always possible to accomplish everything you set out to do, but I'm always willing to take that chance. Again, the real question is whether or not what I'm doing is important in the overall scheme of things.

20. Question: Why would I hire you?
    Answer: It is very likely that many of the other people

who are applying for this job have approximately the same background and skills that I have. But I doubt that anyone has the same interest in the job that I have. And I also doubt that the others are as _ _ _ _ _ _ _ _ _ _ (motivated, hard working, thorough, creative, concerned about the environment, dependable, etc.) as I am. So, I guess my answer is that I'm extremely interested in this position and that I believe my _ _ _ _ _ _ _ _ _ _ (work ethic, motivation, thoroughness, creativity, etc.) will make me successful in performing the job.

21. Question: In what ways do you think you can make a contribution to our company?
    Answer: First, I think my skill level in the field of _ _ _ _ _ _ _ _ (Engineering, Sales, Accounting, Management, etc.) is higher than most other people. Because of this, I can save you time and money by being particularly productive. Second, because I believe I am more interested in the job than most others, I will be more highly motivated to do the best possible job. Third, (if appropriate), my experience in this line of work will enable me to bring a broad perspective to the job. So, the answer to your question is that I'll contribute productivity and a broad perspective because of my motivation and experience.

22. Question: What qualities do you think a successful _ _ _ _ _ _ should possess?
    Answer: First, I think he should be a team player. Unless he can see the broad picture and cooperate with others for the good of the organization, he won't be much good to you. Second, I think he should be an achiever; someone who will get the job done. Third, and perhaps most important, he should be a self-starter who doesn't wait to be told what to do all of the time. And fourth, the person should be dependable. If you can't count on an _ _ _ _ _ _ _ _ _ (accountant, engineer, salesman, etc.) to be dependable, anything else they do is overshadowed.

23. Question: What employment related accomplishment has given you the most satisfaction?
    Answer: Once, when I was working for _ _ _ _ _ _ _ _ _ _ (another company name) I solved a problem involving _ _ _ _ (money, working conditions, a mechanical process, saving

time, etc.). The company was appreciative and it made me feel good to be able to help the company.

24. Question: Why did you select your college or university?
    Answer: As you may know, _ _ _ _ _ _ _ _ _ (name of school) is well known for its _ _ _ _ _ _ _ _ _ (College of Business, Department of Accounting, School of Nursing, etc.). I shopped around but _ _ _ _ _ _ _ _ (name of school) was my first choice, and I'm glad I did because I got a first-rate education in _ _ _ _ _ _ _ _ _ (Business, Accounting, Nursing, etc.).

25. Question: Do you have any plans to go back to school for additional training or education?
    Answer: I think the most valuable employees are those who continue to develop themselves, particularly in these days and times when updated skills are so necessary in _ _ _ _ _ _ _ _ _ (accounting, engineering, etc.).

You have probably noticed that the proposed answers are very generic and avoid specifics. This is recommended for two basic reasons. First, my experience tells me that the more in-depth you are in your answers, the more likely you will get into trouble. This goes against your natural inclination to be straightforward and detailed about your successes and failures. Still, when you get into specifics, you run the risk of saying something that will offend the interviewer or cause him or her to disqualify you.

Second, candid and direct answers are hard to generate on the spur of the moment. Few of us are so glib that we can improvise on a theme without preparation. The net effect is that we say things like, "Well, I think, uh . . . I uh . . .," or "Gee, that's a tough question," or even, "I don't know I suppose I chose communication as a major by accident . . . I guess." You can insist that you are more clever than this and that you can handle yourself in employment interviews without extensive preparation. But why take a chance in the name of vanity? Preparation for these open-ended questions will avoid any possible problems.

The Closed-Ended Questions

Closed-ended questions are much more directive and demanding. They discount your opinion and ask for specific facts. You can't claim uncertainty or an unclear recollection. In short, you must be reasonably straightforward. But that does not mean you have to trap yourself.

It isn't often that you will run into these types of questions. Still, it is best that you prepare for them anyway. The 10 closed-ended questions that follow include answers that you can tailor to your own needs.

1. Question: Have you ever been fired from a job? Yes or no? Explain.
   Answer: No. There has never been any reason for an employer to discharge me.

   or

   Answer: Yes. But it was a question of mutual respect. I had done everything I could for _ _ _ _ _ _ _ _ _ _ (name of company). My superior and I had decided that I would be more valuable to another organization. But I want to say that I admire and respect the company and I learned a great deal about _ _ _ _ _ _ _ _ _ _ (accounting, selling, engineering, managing, etc.) while I worked there.

2. Question: Do you like to work under pressure? Yes or no? Explain.
   Answer: Yes. Of course, it depends on the kind of pressure but as a rule I would have to answer that I do. I find that pressure tends to improve my performance because it increases my determination to get the job done. I feel that I am a self-starter but pressure gives me that extra incentive or push that we all need from time to time.

3. Question: Do you know how to use or operate a _ _ _ _ _ _ _ _ (typewriter, computer, drill press, the 3 C's of selling, SWOT analysis, etc.)? Yes or no? Explain.
   Answer: Yes. I used _ _ _ _ _ _ _ _ _ _ (a typewriter, computer, drill press, etc.) in my last job and became very familiar with it. I also found that I did quite well with it and came to enjoy using it.

   or

   Answer: No. But I am intrigued with the _ _ _ _ _ _ _ _ and would certainly welcome the challenge of mastering it. And if that would involve training, I would welcome that too.

4. Question: How much money do you want to make this year?

Question: Exactly how much of a starting _ _ _ _ _ _ _ _ _ (salary, hourly wage, etc.) are you looking for? Explain.

Answer: Money is important to me, of course, but there are other things too, including job satisfaction and the feeling that I have accomplished something important. So it is hard for me to put a figure on those parts of the job. The only sensible answer I can think of is that I will get what I deserve and I would trust a company like yours to recognize the value in an employee.

5. Question: Have you held a position of leadership or supervision in any organization? Explain.

Answer: Yes. I was a _ _ _ _ _ _ _ _ _ (supervisor, manager, etc.) in my last job. I find _ _ _ _ _ _ _ _ _ very challenging and rewarding.

Answer: No. Circumstances have never presented themselves in a way that would allow me to assume a leadership role, but I look forward to the day when that will be possible. I know I would find such a position challenging and rewarding.

6. Question: Are you seeking employment in a company of a certain size? Yes or no? Explain.

Answer: Yes. I would like to work for a company that offers me a chance to develop and use all of my skills. I feel a large company can give me that chance.

7. Question: What do you think is the most important asset for a _ _ _ _ _ _ _ _ _ (manager, salesperson, etc.)? Is it: Technical ability? The ability to work with others? Being a self-starter? Why?

Answer: I would say the ability to work with others, because, if you can't work with other people, all the technical competence and personal drive in the world isn't going to help much. Organizations are made up of people, after all, and you have to interact with others if you want to use your drive and skill to the best advantage.

8. Question: How many times were you late for work last year? How many personal or sick days did you take last year? Explain.

Answer: I didn't take any time off and I was never late. It is simply not like me to take personal days off. It seems to me that if an employee is being paid for a day's work he or she should be there to do it on time.

or

Answer: I was _ _ _ _ _ _ _ _ _ _ (sick or late) _ _ _ _ _ _ _ _ times last year due to _ _ _ _ _ _ _ _ _ _ (sudden illness, undependable car, construction on the interstate, etc.). But the problem was temporary and I don't anticipate this difficulty will occur any longer. I believe in a full day's work for a full day's pay and I've always felt guilty about being _ _ _ _ _ _ _ _ _ (late or sick).

9. Question: With how many other organizations have you interviewed? What are their names?

Answer: This is the only interview I have had so far. I am being extremely selective.

or

Answer: I have had _ _ _ _ _ interviews so far. They have included _ _ _ _ _ _ _ _ _ _ (names of companies). I am being extremely selective in this job search. I must point out though, that I am extremely interested in this job.

10. Question: What was the last book you read? Why did you read it?

Answer: The last book I read was _ _ _ _ _ _ _ _ _ _ (name of book). Although I enjoy recreational or leisure reading, I believe it is important to keep up in one's profession or trade and that is where I spend most of my reading time.

As you can see, questions of this sort can be demanding in the sense that they demand that you think on your feet. You can't prepare for them as well because you don't know what they are likely to ask. Beyond that, they require hard data rather than simple opinion.

Still, as I said, you will not run into questions of this sort very often, so you need not be too concerned. If you do, you should be cautious, of course, but you should be as honest as possible. The information obtained through such questions can frequently be checked and if you distort the truth it may trip you up and cause you not to be hired. Nevertheless, you must constantly try to protect yourself from disclosing more than necessary, and by preparing your answers in advance as much as possible.

Leaving The Interview

It is extremely important that you make a good impression when you leave the interview. Accordingly, you would be wise to consider the following suggestions:

1. **Never ask how you did.** First of all, the interviewer will probably not tell you the truth because he can't for one reason or another. Second, he may feel embarrassed because he has to reject you. Finally, you may also put him in the awkward position of having to make an immediate decision that could backfire.

2. **Always express your interest in the position.** You should leave the prospective employer with the clear impression that you really want the job. You can indicate this by saying, "I want you to understand that I am really interested in the position as _ _ _ _ _," or "I just want to let you know that the job sounds very challenging, just the sort of position I've been looking for." You don't want to overdo it, but your enthusiasm might be the factor that tips the scale in your direction.

3. **Always ask for a time commitment regarding a choice.** It is important to you to find out how long the selection process is going to take so that you can make other plans accordingly. More often than not, you can expect the employer to be somewhat vague on this point, but whatever information you get will be better than not knowing anything at all. It is simply a question of asking when they will make a decision and when and how you will be notified.

4. **Don't ask about wages or benefits.** If the employer has not raised the issue of compensation, he or she has his or her reasons. There will be time for discussions on this topic if and when you are offered the job. However, if you raise the question yourself, it may appear that this is all you care about and very few employers will hire someone who appears to be interested in nothing but money and vacations.

5. **Always thank the employer for interviewing you.** This may seem like common sense but I have interviewed hundreds of people who acted as though they did me a big

favor by showing up in the first place, and I have never hired such a person. You, after all, are the one who wants the favor of being hired. It only stands to reason that you should thank the person for considering you. But even if you don't quite feel this way, thanking the employer will impress him or her much more than if you assume an arrogant attitude.

FOLLOWING UP

Once the interview is over, it is a good idea to take several other steps.

A Thank You Letter

You would be surprised about how effective a follow-up letter can be. While it may not change the employer's mind who has already decided to hire someone else, it could mean the difference between getting or not getting the job if the employer hasn't yet made up his or her mind. Beyond this, he or she may consider you for another job.

A letter of this sort makes you stand out from the other candidates; it also reinforces the notion that you want the job. Finally, it tells the employer that you are a professional who approaches the job search in a professional manner.

Of course, you must be sure that the letter appears to be sincere. It must also be written in such a way that it sounds appreciative without sounding too subservient. The following letter is offered as a example:

Mr/Ms. _ _ _ _ _ _ _ _ _ _:
Thank you for the opportunity to meet with you last _ _ _ _ _ _ _ _ _ _.
The interview was very informative and the position as a _ _ _ _ _ _ _ _
sounds quite _ _ _ _ _ _ _ _ _ (interesting, challenging, fascinating, etc.). If you should need any additional information, please feel free to contact me at _ _ _ _ _ _ _ _ _ (phone number).
Again, thank you for talking with me. I would welcome the opportunity to work for _ _ _ _ _ _ _ _ _ (name of company).
Sincerely,

A Follow-Up Phone Call

A follow-up phone call should never be made unless you have first sent a letter such as the one indicated above. Also, it should never be made more than once. The purpose of the call is twofold: first, it tells the prospective employer that you really want the job; second, it is a way of checking on your status.

The advantage of the call over simply sending the letter is that you get immediate feedback. The disadvantage is that it may seem pushy. It is a question of understanding the situation and deciding whether a phone call is appropriate. If it is, the call can be another way to encourage the employer to hire you.

Negotiating a Wage or Salary

VERY FEW JOBS HAVE A WAGE OR SALARY THAT IS WRITTEN IN stone. Although the employer may make a claim that the top wage or salary is fixed, if he or she really wants to hire you, you are in the driver's seat and in a position to demand more. However, you must understand the fundamentals of negotiation in order to get what you want. A simple arrogant insistence, for instance, may put the employer in a defensive position and you could actually lose money or even the job itself in the process.

UNDERSTANDING THE NEGOTIATION PROCESS

The first step in negotiating a raise is to understand that the employer has an ego and that he will react very negatively if he feels he is being threatened or blackmailed. Your intention may be innocent enough, but if he thinks that you are trying to push him around he may go so far as to withdraw any previous offer he has made, and send you packing.

I watched this exact thing happen some time ago. I had interviewed a man for an executive position with a medical supply company. Although he was very qualified, he was very arrogant with me so I told my superior that I did not want to hire him. My boss, however, overruled my objection and personally entered into direct negotiations with him. Apparently the man could have had the job at the salary he wanted (much higher than normal for that position) because my boss was so impressed with his credentials. But the man was so arrogant and demanding during the negotiations that my boss threw him out of his office!

The point is that everyone has an ego abuse threshold, and there is no real standard other than common sense to determine what that is for the person that you are talking to. However, a basic rule of thumb is to ask yourself how much you yourself would take before you would reject the candidate and withdraw your offer.

The second step is recognizing that you must focus on what the person *really* wants rather than what he says he wants. You may be surprised to learn that these two things are usually not the same. Perhaps a simple example would prove useful.

Jack has applied for a job with a collection agency as a sales manager. He has an impressive track record and after being offered the job, the following conversation takes place:

Jack: How much are you willing to pay?
Employer: Well, we were thinking somewhere in the neighborhood of $40,000.
Jack: You have to be kidding. I wouldn't take it for less than $60,000.
Employer: We've never paid anyone that kind of money for that job.

Now, each party has stated his position and as a consequence each is at a significant stalemate. Neither side is likely to be willing to change his mind because he does not want to appear to be weak, or to be giving in. And as long as each insists on his respective positions, there can be no progress.

If Jack is smart, he will analyze the situation and try to figure out what the employer really wants. Is he trying to save money for his company or is he sticking to policy? Maybe it is something else entirely different such as his ego? By asking himself these questions he begins to deal with the real issue behind the stated intent—that the employer does not want to feel that he is being pushed around. By focusing on the man's ego-threat he could then begin to negotiate more effectively.

Jack: I know that this position doesn't normally command $60,000 but I bring a lot of success with me to this job. Given your broad experience, do you really believe that's all I'm worth? What do you think would be an equitable salary given all of my experience?

Here Jack has done two important things. To begin with, he has complimented the employer which addresses the real issue of the man's ego. Also, he has opened the negotiation to possible compromise thereby eliminating the stalemate. If the employer responds that he still is not willing to pay more than $40,000, Jack should try to establish some objective way to determine what his salary should be. And that is the next step in effective salary negotiation.

For instance, Jack could suggest that they scan the local newspaper together to see what the average salary is for a person of his experience and success. Or he might propose that they contact an executive recruiter to establish an objective standard for a salary base. Finally, Jack could suggest that they examine each aspect of the job to establish its real value to the company. Once the objective standard is set, negotiations become easier because the employer's ego is safe—he no longer feels the threat of being pushed—and Jack's sense of his own worth is protected—the fair standard will determine his value once and for all.

Presuming that they agree on the standard, Jack should now try to work out as many options as possible to speed the process along. For example, if $50,000 seems to be the fair salary for the position, how should it be paid out? Is he willing to take $45,000 plus a company car and a stock option plan? Would he accept $40,000 plus a substantial semiannual bonus? The point is, the more options he has, the more successful he will be because: 1) he seems flexible and willing to compromise; 2) he can move around the employer's objections more easily; and 3) he can respond to the employer's suggestions more effectively. Without these options, Jack and the employer are likely to wind up in a stalemate again.

One other aspect of the option package that Jack should bring to the negotiation is to try to have other offers when he negotiates with the employer. While this is not always possible, if he can arrange it, he is in a much stronger position to bargain. First, the other offers will keep him from panicking and accepting the initial $40,000 offer out of desperation. Second, he can explain to the employer that he has another offer and that he must weigh both of them before making his final decision. This last point, of course, puts pressure on the employer to meet Jack's terms.

SALARY NEGOTIATION STRATEGIES

Once you understand the basic process of effective salary negotiation (respecting the other person's ego, developing fair standards, and creating as many options as possible), you must then understand that there are certain strategies that you can use which will enhance your position even further.

The first strategy is to always get as much as you can when you are first hired because any salary increases in the future will normally be based on your entry level package. If you "low-ball" your initial salary package in order to get the job, with the idea that you can make up any discrepancy later on, you are deluding yourself. Take our friend Jack, for instance. If he takes the position for a straight $40,000 on the false assumption that he will get substantial increases once the company realizes his worth, it may be years before he even begins to approach the $60,000 he originally had in mind. Even if he got a 15 percent increase in his salary each year for five years in a row (a *very* optimistic scenario), he still would not be making the money he wanted at the outset.

A second strategy is not to discuss your salary requirements too early in the negotiation process. It is to your disadvantage to do so because the employer cannot possibly know what you are worth to his company until he has taken sufficient time to learn about your total value to him. Also, once he is finally convinced that he really wants to hire you, you are in a much better position to negotiate for more money.

Most employers are aware of the strategy and some will try to derail you by offering you a salary figure right away. As is indicated in chapter 10, be very wary of the immediate offers. The reasons he might do this aside, it puts you in a dangerous position if you respond favorably to the premature offer. The primary damage to you has to do with an old but true adage that, he who commits first to a position in any type of financial bargaining is normally the winner. If you seem willing to consider that figure, you are putting automatic limits on any future possibilities. Also, it puts you in the difficult position of making an immediate decision without having the real opportunity to analyze it. Therefore, if the employer says to you, "This job pays $40,000. When can you start?" during the early moments of the initial interview try to put him off in the most diplomatic way you can. You might say, "Well, I wonder if we can wait to discuss money until I know more about the job. By the way, did you say that this job . . .?" Or you might counter by saying, "Money isn't really my primary concern right now, I'm more interested in making a significant contribution. Did I understand you to say that this job . . .?"

Another approach some employers take is to ask you almost at the outset how much you are expecting before they have made any sort of firm offer to you. They frequently do this to make their choice of candidate as simple as possible. If you want too much money, they can dismiss you right away and avoid the rest of what could be a difficult interview. The question, "How much money are you looking for?" is an attempt to put the burden of proof on you. In any case, your response should be the same as was indicated above; that is, avoid an immediate affirmative response at any cost.

If, however, he will not take "no" for an answer, give him the broadest possible range that you can such as, "Well, I'd like to earn $45,000 to $60,000 this year depending on my level of responsibility." The idea here is to increase your options and adjust your acceptable figure once you know what the job actually entails.

Some employers play another game of which you should be aware. They offer you the job *without* mentioning what the salary is. They do this to get a commitment from you before money is discussed. In effect, they are dangling the proverbial carrot-on-the-stick before your eyes. At last you have landed the job that you want, but once you accept it they are in the driver's seat and you have lost the negotiation. Your natural inclination is to accept the offer because you are so happy with the prospect of working for this company or doing the kind of work that they are offering.

The best way to handle the offer without mention of salary, is to say something like the following: "I am very grateful for the offer to join the Ajax company but so far we haven't discussed a salary. While money is a secondary issue here, it is important and I really can't commit myself until we come to terms. It seems to me that with my experience and success in this field, I should be worth approximately $55,000 to $60,000." After saying that, remain silent and avoid the temptation to say anything more. Now, you are in the driver's seat. After all, he has already committed himself to hiring you. Now he has to figure out how to get you to join his company; and you, in turn, have established a first commitment posture.

One final and very simple strategy for salary negotiation is to split the difference. If the employer offers $40,000 and you were thinking in terms of $60,000 it may be in your best interest to exercise an option such as offering to accept it for $50,000; However, never do this unless you hold out for some additional income tied to performance.

In the final analysis, salary negotiation is just another part of the employment interviewing game. If you follow the advice in this chapter you will be surprised at how easy it is to get more money and benefits than you ever thought possible.

How to Interview When Changing Jobs

JUST 15 YEARS AGO, THE TYPICAL EMPLOYEE STAYED WITH ONE company 10 years before moving on to another position. Today the average tenure is 3.5 years. People are changing jobs at an increasing rate because once they gain a skill or experieince, they are usually more valuable than their employer will admit. Recognizing this, they move on to other positions with other companies that are willing to pay a premium for their talents. In addition to this, many employees realize that they are dead-ended in their jobs due to technology or retrenchment. For these and other reasons, people are moving from job to job in increasing numbers.

Unfortunately, not all of these transitions are really successful. One reason is that the candidate is too frank. Another is that the individual is not really sure of what he or she is looking for. In this chapter, we are going to examine each of these problems in detail.

BEING TOO FRANK

There is an old saying that you can never be too honest. I will not debate ethical standards here, but I will say that sometimes people undermine their own credibility by saying things that need not be said. For instance, if your manager has asked you to forge a document (claiming greater sales than you actually attained, or claiming profits never realized), you might decide to quit. While this is quite laudable, and should evoke strong positive responses from the potential employer, it could result in the opposite effect. Admitting that you are quitting for this reason may be true, but to the potential employer it might also seem disloyal or ungrateful.

The trick here is to modify your response by saying that you simply want to work for a company that more closely matches your own business interests and style, or that you are leaving because your present situation does not offer you what you need.

Or perhaps it is a question of being passed over at promotion time. Again, if you show a bitter attitude toward your present employer it will prejudice your case. It is much better to simply say that you are looking for new opportunities.

THE PROBLEM WITH EMPLOYER REFERENCES

If you are changing jobs, you might not want to list your present employer as a reference unless you are leaving on the best of terms and your boss wants to help you find something new. In that case, you have no problem with employer references. That, of course, is seldom the question. Most people who are changing jobs are very reluctant to list their present employer or superior as references, then, because they have not even told them that they are leaving.

The simplest way to deal with this difficulty is to indicate on your resume that you are sending it in strict confidence. Many people suggest this approach but it may not work. Once, when I was changing jobs, I tried this method and it got me nowhere. I have never had such a poor response to a resume. When I eliminated this phrase, I had much better luck.

Apparently, when you indicate that your resume or application is confidential, it makes you look suspicious. It seems to "red flag" you as a problem person who should not be trusted. After all, it might be interpreted as an attempt to hide something.

A better approach is to simply indicate where you are working and take a chance. Studies show that most potential employers do not check references, so it is very unlikely that they will call your present employer.

Another approach is to give personal references rather than listing former employers. If you do this before they ask you for what they want, it may take the momentum out of their efforts. If the potential employer insists on business or employment references, you can always refer to the job you had before your present employment. If asked for a reference from a current employer, you can always say that you do not want them to know that you are leaving. Most potential employers will respect this wish.

FOCUSING YOUR SIGHTS

One of the biggest difficulties in changing jobs is focusing your sights on exactly what you want to do and where you want to do it. Do you want to continue what you are presently doing in another organization or do you intend to change careers? Depending on your answer to this question, you will have a little or a lot of research to do. Let us begin with just changing locations.

If you simply want to work for another company, you should begin by researching the possibilities. The most obvious starting place is the local newspaper. The telephone directory classified section may prove useful as well. There you will find the names of all companies doing business that relate to your present occupation. You can then make a list of those that interest you based on their reputation. If you don't know much about them, you can call or visit your local Chamber of Commerce and ask for specific information about a company's size, sales volume, etc. Then it is a question of calling on the company and arranging to fill out an application or scheduling an interview.

Then there is the networking process discussed in chapter 3. The difficulty with networking, however, might be that you might want to keep your move confidential; in that case, networking would be foolish since the process requires that you let the world know that you are looking for another position.

If you want a change of scenery and think that a move to another city might interest you, you might consider reviewing the *Wall Street Journal*, the *National Business Employment Weekly*, *The New York Times*, or a newspaper from the city in question. Many of these are available free of charge in your local public library. You can also write to the newspaper and ask for a limited subscription.

Now, let us assume that you want to change your career. It now becomes a question of keying in on the kinds of jobs that are of interest to you. Glancing through the classified ads in your local newspaper will give you a fair idea of the range of possibilities in your area. You will want to make a list of any openings that seem attractive. Don't be too concerned at this point that you don't have the skills or training required. Those can always be gained, within reason of course.

If you are an accountant and you see ads for over-the-road truck drivers, training to become a truck driver can be obtained through various schools. If you are a salesperson and you want to be an accountant it might mean years in school but the moment you make the decision to start, you are on your way. If that prospect seems too long-term, you might decide to settle for an auxiliary job such as becoming a bookkeeper. The point is that you should make as broad a list as possible and then weigh various factors such as: 1) the skills required; 2) the time it will take to acquire them if you don't presently have them; 3) the income you can expect to earn; 4) the cost of training; 5) the personal advantage that you think you will gain; and 6) the personal disadvantages the job might hold.

Once you have made your list and narrowed down your career choices, you should ask people in the field about the positive and negative aspects of the new occupation or profession. A colleague of mine at a university changed from being a PhD philosophy professor to becoming a computer expert. He decided that university teaching did not pay enough money for his growing family so he did the research I have mentioned. After talking to professionals in the field, he discovered that computer engineering was a very high paying job. Accordingly, he went to a neighboring university and began taking computer courses. When he decided he had enough training, he applied for a job with a large firm and was hired. He then went on to get a Masters of Business Administration.

Another avenue for making a job change is to contact a career counselor. They are especially useful if you have an idea of what you want to do. Some are better than others, but they can help you determine what is right for you. You will find them listed under "Career and Vocational Counseling" in your telephone directory. If you decide to choose this avenue you can make things a lot easier for yourself and save money by limiting the possibilities. Normally, these agencies give you aptitude or psychological tests and then discuss the range of your potentials. The more you have thought about your specific interests by doing your own basic research in advance, the quicker and cheaper it will be for you.

Finally, there is the question of deciding at what level job you are willing to start. Whenever you decide to make a job change, you must face the fact that people and their professions are valued differently from company to company. For example, a person with a masters degree who teaches at a two-year community college or junior college is highly valued and highly paid. However, if he or she switches to a four-year university, he or she will generally start at the bottom because he or she does not have a PhD. In some organizations, an engineer is regarded as one of the company's most important assets; in other organizations, an engineer is seen as little more than someone who helps to maintain systems. On a similar point, if you change careers, you will be a novice and you will probably have to start at an entry level position. For instance, an inexperienced truck driver, no matter how much training he or she has had, is not as valuable as an experienced person who knows how to avoid mistakes. So you may have to resign yourself to starting at the bottom of the ladder.

CHANGING YOUR STYLE

When you change jobs, you frequently have to change your style (the way you look and act), because no two organizations are exactly the same. In some instances, the changes you will have to make will be minor. In others, the necessary changes will be significant.

Of course, you must demonstrate the right style from the first moment you are interviewed. Therefore, you should follow the advice in chapter 2, and prepare yourself accordingly by looking and sounding as though you are a good match for the corporate, division, or department with which you will be working.

If you are changing careers, creating the right style may be a bit more involved. For one thing, you have to research the particular company. For another, you must research the preferred style for your new occupation. Accountants, as a rule, tend to act more conservatively than salespeople; university professors are usually more analytical than bartenders; taxi drivers are usually more direct than bank tellers. It does not take a genius to do research of this sort but if you ignore this aspect of preparation, you are making a major mistake. The way you look and act during the interview process is generally more important than your actual skill level.

GAINING NEW SKILLS

It was already pointed out that there are schools that train truck drivers. Obviously, there are also schools that train teachers, models, and everything in between. However, the cost and quality of these institutions varies widely and should be checked carefully.

One of the best ways to investigate a training academy or school is to ask the placement office (most have them) about their success in placing graduates. Demand records, numbers, and anything else that will document their track record; after all, you are the customer and you have a right to know what you are buying. Also, ask for the names and phone numbers of recent graduates so that you can talk to them about their training and subsequent job success.

Surprisingly, the local public school system can be a very useful source of vocational or professional training. Local junior colleges and universities can also provide you with important training and education. Usually, and this may seem odd, they are much cheaper than private institutions.

Whatever you do, avoid the temptation to take the typical correspondence school training. While some training of this sort may be legitimate, and possibly useful, the job seeker should beware of outrageous claims such as, "You too can be making big bucks in just two weeks," or "Join the glamorous world of radio announcing . . . train in your own home with these incredible video tapes."

Whatever you do, realize that your time, money, and energy is an investment. You can spend your resources wisely or foolishly. It is a matter of careful investigation and common sense.

RE-THINKING YOUR RESUME

The most successful job seekers are those that change their resume according to the job for which they are applying. A single resume may not cover all of your job interests or possibilities. Recognizing this, you should examine your present resume with an eye to your new job interests. For example, if you are a production supervisor and you want a job in public relations, you should stress your public contact experience. It becomes a matter of interpretation.

Let's look at a revised edition of a resume on page 75 that we reviewed earlier in chapter 2.

Obviously, a few word changes can make a significant difference. Beginning with the objective, you should indicate exactly what you are looking for. This establishes from the outset that you believe you are qualified for the position, and that you have an entry

EDWARD BLAKE

1423 University Blvd.   Birmingham, AL.   412-711-7006

OBJECTIVE	To obtain an entry level public relations position with a progressive and dynamic organization.
EDUCATION	University of Alabama BA 1978 Course work included communications, writing, human relations.
EXPERIENCE	Doblin Industries: Internal personnel relations; direct employee contact and supervision; 1978 to present
	Parker Drugs: customer service representative, clerk, 1977 to 1978
	Summer Youth Camp: Assistant Counselor, 1975
MEMBERSHIPS	Rotary Club (Northside); membership chairperson; public relations committee

level background. Next, instead of claiming an "English" major, the candidate stresses writing, communications, and human relations. After all, English majors learn to write, study the art of communication, and come to understand people as they research novels, short stories, and poetry. By the same token, successful production supervisors must learn to deal with a variety of people in a positive way in order to get the job done. This could easily be described in terms of public relations. So, it is a question of using the right words to describe your interests and your training and experience. It is not manipulative to re-define yourself; it is describing yourself according to your interests.

Some years ago, I was asked to become the volunteer editor of a magazine of a private club that I belonged to. When I was approached, it was assumed that because I was a writer, a university professor, and a business consultant, I had the necessary qualifications to do the job. True, I had edited a few newsletters for private industry, but this was a major undertaking involving everything from writing, to layout, to publication. When they asked for my resume, I indicated that I was an undergraduate communications major (a writer), had experience as a communication/business professor (a knowledgable and experienced communicator, organizor and businessman), and that I was an editor (I had been involved in editing the newsletters). I landed the position, and while providing an element of leadership and direction, I learned as much as I could about sophisticated publishing.

All it requires is a little imagination and self-confidence to rethink your resume. Whatever you do, you must recognize that one resume will seldom be enough; you must target your credentials to the position you are seeking.

9

Dealing with the College Recruiter

FOR THOSE OF YOU JUST GRADUATING, OR ABOUT TO GRADUATE from college, the college recruiter can be of particular interest. More and more corporations are recruiting their management trainees and other entry level employees directly from the campus. Generally, they work through the college or university placement office.

As a rule, the system works like this; the company involved contacts the school; they then arrange to come to the campus to interview prospective candidates; students are notified of the impending visit and they schedule interviews with the representatives of the various corporations.

PREPARING FOR THE INTERVIEW

Preparing for an interview with the college recruiter is not much different from preparing for any other interview. As was indicated in Chapter 2, you must prepare in advance by finding out as much as possible about the corporation, memorize answers to commonly asked questions, and dress in a professional manner. However, this situation involves some special considerations.

First, the college employment recruiter usually has a very basic mission. He or she is to find the "best" college graduates for the organization. But what is "best" is often a question of individual, subjective evaluation based on confusing criteria. For example, the recruiter frequently has very little specific information about the job involved. As a rule, he or she is asked to recruit candidates on the basis of broad qualifications such as a college degree in accounting, a "B+" average, an outgoing personality, leadership ability, interest in research, etc. Now, there is no way that a recruiter can determine much from a single interview, particularly when the criteria are so broad and so subjective. Although, it is easy enough to check up on a person's recorded and official background, how does a person determine leadership ability in a single interview?

The fact that a person is president of an organization may only mean that the person is politically astute. Research is clear in this area. Leadership and political ability do not go hand in hand. Politicians are generally popular with those with whom they work. Leaders, on the other hand, are generally *unpopular* with those that they lead because they have to make difficult choices that don't coincide with each of their constituents wishes. They are, however, respected. So even the fact that an individual has held office in a prominent organization, does not mean that the candidate is a leader.

It is even more difficult to determine whether a person has an "outgoing personality." The best the recruiter can hope to do is make a very subjective judgment about what he or she sees in the candidate. If the candidate seems sure of him or herself, for example, because he or she has a firm handshake and speaks without hesitation, the candidate may be viewed as "outgoing." If the candidate is assertive and speaks his or her mind, he or she may be perceived as "outgoing." The recruiter can only judge this and other traits on the basis of your behavior.

The college employment recruiter faces a second special problem. The students that he or she interviews have no employment track record. Or, if they do, the jobs that they have had while going to school seldom relate to the position for which they are being interviewed. Somehow, the recruiter must decide whether the candidate will be able to perform the job effectively and efficiently. The only way he or she can really do this is by guessing!

These factors put you in the driver's seat because most of what the interviewer knows about you is controlled by you. In preparation then, first, ask the placement office at your school what they think the company is looking for. The following checklist should prove useful:

1. Is the company:
   conservative____
   progressive____
   traditional____
   modern, futuristic____
   growth oriented____
   status quo oriented____
   known for quality____
   known for customer service____
   known as an industry leader____
   high participative, team oriented____
   hierarchical, authoritarian____
   human relations oriented____
2. Are they looking for a person who is:
   high-energy____
   a team player____
   a self starter____
   a planner____
   analytical____
   assertive____
   aggressive____
   outgoing____
   thorough____
   a high-producer____
3. What kind of major do they prefer:
   accounting____
   marketing____
   management____
   engineering____
   physics____
   biology____
   art____
   communication____
   public relations____
   sociology____
   economics____
   political science____
   psychology____
   computer information systems____
   nursing____
   other____

4. What sort of interviews do they conduct:
    formal____
    informal____
    structured____
    unstructured____
    standardized questions____
    improvised questions____

5. What kind of wage and benefit package do they generally offer:
    a. wage spread____to____/hr or week
    b. benefits:
        life insurance____
        medical insurance____
        dental insurance____
        vacation days____
        bonuses____
        stock options____
        profit sharing____

6. Is the position in question:
    entry level____
    management trainee____
    fast-track promotion____
    high stress____
    routine____
    creative____
    local____
    regional____
    national____
    involve traveling____
    other____

Believe it or not, the typical university placement office can answer these questions. The problem is simply that most students don't know enough to ask them. Obviously, they can be of significant value in preparing your response to the interview.

Assuming the worst scenario, that the placement office can't or won't answer the above questions, there are other ways to find out the answers in order to prepare appropriate responses.

One suggestion is to make sure that you are one of the last people to be interviewed. The reason for this is that you can contact your fellow students who have already been interviewed and ask them what you can expect. Normally, they will be glad to tell you what you need to know.

Another suggestion is to contact alumni who presently or formerly worked for the company. Either the placement office or the alumni office of the university should have the names of people that you can contact.

Finally, if you have tried everything else, you can always call the recruiter before the interview and ask some of the questions. It takes nerve and a lot of self confidence to do this, but you must get the information. The point is that you can't effectively prepare for the interview if you don't have any information. At the very least, you can always follow the general advice offered earlier in the book.

RESPONDING TO THE RECRUITER

In preparing for this book, I conducted a number of interviews with college recruiters from national and local organizations. Their responses to my questions about the interview process were not unexpected or inconsistent with anything previously presented.

To begin with, you must understand that the college recruitment process involves two different types of interviews: the generic "management trainee" interview; and the "job specific" interview. Let's begin with the generic "management trainee" interview.

The Management Trainee Interview

The prime criteria for acceptance or rejection in this situation is your "personality", reflected through your "presentation skills," and your so-called "physical characteristics." One person I talked with admitted, confidentially, that the candidate who "looked" the best would probably be hired by his firm.

In interview situations such as this, your looks are typically more important than your specific skills since the organization may wish to place you in nearly any job. What they are looking for is a so-called cultural match. In other words, what they are trying to do is to match the personality of the person that they hire with the overriding philosophy of the organization. For instance, the company may be one that stresses teamwork, sharing, and cooperation so they will try to find new employees who will be able to flourish in that environment.

As a rule, they will qualify in the interview by asking you prepared, general questions, at the beginning and then seeing how you respond. Then, the interviewer will ask you spontaneous questions based on your reactions to the original questions. This will continue for 30 minutes or so and then the interview will end on what one recruiter I talked to called a "warm note."

If you get to the point of actually being interviewed by most recruiters, there is every reason to believe that they will end up offering you a position sometime later. As one recruiter put it, "Usually, when I decide to interview a student, I have a pretty good idea that he or she has the necessary skills. For one thing, if I have asked the placement office to schedule business majors, I know in advance that they have the necessary business course background I want. For another, I always tell the placement office to schedule only seniors with a 2.5 (B+) average. So I know they are reasonably bright and capable. "Frankly," she concluded, "I find very few that I can weed out." It becomes a question of matching the candidate to the company, in general, and in management trainee interviews the college recruiter is authorized to make the final hiring decision him or herself. The recruiter simply tells the new employee's boss that he or she has hired a person who will begin to work on a particular date.

It should be clear to the reader that this situation is ideal for the candidate. Since you can control your answers, even prepare and rehearse them in advance, you can also control the direction the conversation takes.

If there is a danger here, it is that in the informal interchange it may be very tempting to relax and make off-the-cuff remarks that leave the wrong impression. Avoid this temptation by sticking to your prepared answers. Again, this type of interview allows you to decide what direction the discussion will take so why not take advantage of the situation?

The Job-Specific Interview

This interview differs from the management trainee interview because the recruiter is more interested in your specific skills. Usually, the recruiter has been asked by the hiring manager to find a candidate with special training or experience.

In the best situations, the skills are drawn from a job description that profiles the tasks to be performed and the training needed to accomplish the tasks. In the worst situations, the hiring manager simply tells the recruiter to find a "good" accountant. In the latter case, the recruiter may not have any idea of what constitutes a "good" accountant. Even if the recruiter asks, the description may be faulty. As a consequence, he or she is less likely to find an effective match for the hiring manager.

In any case, the recruiter will normally approach this interview in much the same way he or she does the management trainee interview, which leaves you in control. However, there is one major difference; because the recruiter has a list of the qualifications he or she is looking for, he or she will ask you questions related to these qualifications. For instance, he or she may ask you how much experience you have with a particular process, or a particular type of machinery. If you don't know the answers, it is best to admit so since he or she will probably see through any attempts to cover up. However, you can also indicate that you are familiar with something similar, or that you would welcome the opportunity to learn a new skill.

The better answer is to prepare in advance for the job-specific interview. If you are applying for a position as an engineer, you should try to find out as much about the job as possible before the interview so that you can familiarize yourself with the processes used in that application at that company. If you are applying for a job as a salesperson, you should know as much as possible about the company's products and services.

One other major difference is that you can expect to go through a round-robin interview at some point. As was mentioned earlier, the recruiter does not actually select the person to be hired. All he or she does is qualify the candidate and send him or her to the hiring manager who will decide whether or not to hire him or her. The hiring manager will, in turn, send the candidate to other people to be interviewed. Let us take the case of our salesman.

The candidate has done his or her homework, qualifies for the job, and is interviewed by the sales manager. The sales manager sends the candidate to the general manager for an interview. Frequently, the candidate is scheduled for a full day of interviews. At some point, our candidate is taken out to lunch where he or she meets others who will supply more information about the specifics of the job. Once again, the danger here (aside from the general problem with round-robin interviews outlined in chapter 3) has to do with relaxing. I have personally seen people make terrible blunders at lunchtime because they believed that the lunch was more or less "off-the-record." Remember, wherever you are with a prospective employer, you are being interviewed, no matter what the setting!

A final difference between the generic and job-specific interview is that in the job-specific interview you may learn of the advantages as well as the disadvantages of the position.

As a rule, once he or she qualifies you, the management trainee recruiter tries to sell the company to you. He tells you wonderful things about the organization and describes the benefits to be gained once you become part of the team. If the job-specific recruiter, knows what he or she is doing, he or she will tell you both sides of the story. It is in his or her best advantage to do so. For one thing, it will reduce the risk of people quitting soon after they are hired. For another, it will reduce the possibility of the recruiter looking as though he or she doesn't know what he or she is doing.

This is not to say that all management trainee interviewers will be deliberately evasive or dishonest. For instance, more often than not, the typical interviewer will have limits set by higher authorities concerning what he or she may tell you. Or, as frequently as not, he or she may not know the real disadvantages that you will face.

10

The Special Problems of Women

IT SHOULD NOT COME AS A SURPRISE TO THE READER THAT WOMEN are still discriminated against in American business. For example, according to very recent findings, women, in general, earn 67% of of what men earn for exactly the same work. For women managers, the situation is even worse. They only earn 54% as much as men. On top of this, most women who are promoted are promoted into service positions that have little or no impact on the real operation of a business. Given the situation, women have to be *very* careful in selecting a position or they may wind up with a dead end or low-paying job despite a lot of promises.

WHAT YOU ARE UP AGAINST

In some ways, women are their own worst enemies in the job market. In recent years, they have downgraded their role as homemaker and they have brought the same negative attitude about themselves with them to the business world. Through the years, this attitude of inferiority has been exploited by many men who work hard to keep women "in their place" because it can mean making handsome profits. Most women have not only gone along with the system, they have actually perpetuated it. Everytime a woman is humiliated into taking a low paying, subservient job, she is telling other women that this situation is a fact of life, and to accept whatever you can get. On top of this, women, as workers today, are sometimes unskilled wives and mothers who have to work to help support their families. In short, they frequently take nearly any job at nearly any wage just to put food on the table. Men by contrast, can be much more choosey. These facts encourage many employers to believe that women can be paid less than men. It is unfair, of course, but it is a reality you will have to face.

Another factor that leads to underpaying women is the myth that they do not need as much money to live on because, if they are single, they do not have to support a family; and, if they are married it is assumed that their income is "extra" money for the family. So, once again they are paid less.

Then there is the problem of playing the "office wife." According to one study, many women like the secretary role because it is little more than a comfortable variation on being a traditional homemaker. Also, a lot of women are convinced that the rough and tumble, high pressure world of business involves too much responsibility and is no place for a woman. They tend to prefer less demanding, more emotionally satisfying roles. The male makes the decision as they support him from a comfortable distance, all the while encouraging the male boss to pamper them and protect them from the cold, harsh world of contemporary business. This worthless stereotype of the roles males and females should play is ridiculous but it is also a comfortable and simplistic way to work things out.

If you doubt the truth of what you have just read, study after study demonstrates that a vast majority of women prefer male bosses. The information is consistent; women tend to feel that men make "better bosses" because they are better businesspeople and are fairer in making decisions and rendering judgements. It has also been established that most women believe men make better leaders, as well, because they are more logical, clear, and precise in guiding the destiny of the organization. By contrast, it is supposed by both males and females that women are too emotional to be trusted with major decisions. There is no reason to believe that any of this is true, but it is an easy way to deal with the complicated process of business in our constantly changing society.

Finally, it is still believed that most women don't really need jobs; that most will eventually get married, have children, and will be supported by a man. This too, is without much foundation, but it is the way most employers still operate. It follows that if women do not need to work, they will probably quit to have children, or move when the husband is transferred, or leave on a whim to do something else. So, many employers argue that women should not be given any real responsibility because they cannot be trusted to stick around.

You would think that the women's liberation movement would have resulted in an improved situation for women at work, but there is little evidence to support this position. In fact, many experts believe the movement created a backlash that has reinforced most of the stereotypes. So, what you are up against is a business world that firmly believes that you do not need much money, that you want to and should play the subservient, safe, traditional roles, that you cannot be trusted to make tough decisions because you are too emotional, and that you will easily quit for any number of reasons.

SELECTING THE RIGHT COMPANY

Even if you are not a feminist, or an active person in the "Women's Movement," you will want to get as much out of your work as possible. Therefore, you will want to select a job that will lead to satisfaction, the highest possible pay, and perhaps, a possibility of promotion.

The first thing to do is to evaluate the organization's track record with women. The claim that the company is "an equal opportunity employer" is a start but it may be more form than substance. The following is a list of questions you may want to consider and evaluate before or during the interview:

- Are women in important, decision-making positions?
- Do they ask sexist questions during the interview?
- Where do most women work (in service or line management positions)?
- Does the pay seem consistent with the industry standard for the job?
- Is this a job that leads to promotions?
- Can this job lead to a transfer to other departments?
- Is this a career path or a dead-end job?
- Is additional training needed to be promoted?

The answers to these questions could save you a lot of grief. Failure to ask these questions may result in disappointment or anger in the future.

Another source of information about a company's track record is the people that you know who work there. This time you can use the networking technique discussed in chapter 3 to find out what you need to know about their hiring, pay, and promotion practices. Still another source of information is any literature you can obtain about the organization such as an annual report or advertising pamphlet or brochure. If there are pictures, are women constantly shown in traditional, supportive, non-authority roles (secretary, clerk, etc.)? Or are they presented doing scientific research or leading a meeting of men? Does the writing stress so-called "traditional values" or does it speak about "progressive thinking" or "new ways of doing things?" These are subtle clues as to how you can expect to be treated in a male-dominated business. Remember, it may sometimes feel comfortable to retreat to stereotyped roles in a business, but it can also prove very expensive in the long run.

RESPONDING TO SEXISM IN THE HIRING PROCESS

No matter how much they try to hide it, most people you will interview with (men and women) will give themselves away if they are sexist. They may make a simple remark such as referring to the female employees as "girls," or they may say that the job is open because "Carol just had a baby and you know how that goes." In both cases, the remarks tell you a lot about the individual you are talking to. In the first instance, referring to women as "girls" is important because it consciously or unconsciously suggests that female workers are children, and/or that female workers are thought of in the stereotypical ways mentioned earlier. In the second instance, the phrase, "you know how that goes" implies that the speaker recognizes and accepts the stereotype of the weak, fragile, undependable female, and/or that Carol probably will not be back because mothers tend to, or should, stay home with their babies. Even a comment that suggests that women are given special favors is a clue. Now, you may be saying to yourself that this is nit-picking, that these words and phrases are common and really meaningless; common, perhaps, but not meaningless. They might be the tip of the discrimination iceberg.

I should point out that one person does not necessarily reflect an entire organization, so the reader should be cautious in assuming too much. On the other hand, he or she may present a very typical example of the presiding corporate philosophy.

Of course, some people do not try to hide their prejudices. The male chauvinist will often say something like, "We don't go for that women's liberation crap around here. We believe that men are men and girls are girls!" Or he may tell an indecent sexist joke or make a lewd remark. It is also entirely possible that an extremely traditional female human resource manager might point out offhand that "the girls in the office are required to wear dresses." In my experience, most employers are not this obvious because they do not want to be sued for breaking the law. Therefore, you will probably have to watch for the small clues like those I have already mentioned.

The Illegal Sexist Questions

As was pointed out in chapter 6, you can expect to face illegal questions of all sorts in most interviews. Often, this is simply ignorance on the part of the interviewer; he or she does not realize that the question is against the law. On the other hand, there is hardly an employer in the United States who does not understand that sexist questions violate Federal and most state laws.

The following is a list of implicit and explicit sexist questions and statements that in one way or another, violate the law:

- Do you intend to get married?
- Are you married?
- Do you intend to have children?
- If you are married, will you quit to follow your husband if he is transferred?
- (A male interviewer) Maybe we could discuss your credentials over dinner at my place?
- I like your legs. What does the rest of you look like?
- Do you believe in dating the boss?
- Do you belong to any feminist clubs or organizations?
- Do you have to work to support your family?
- Are you a feminist?

- What does your husband do for a living?
- Are you divorced, separated, or engaged?
- Are you pregnant?
- Would you miss work because one of your children got sick?
- Why would a good-looking woman like you want a job as a construction engineer?
- Which is more important to you; your potential career or getting married?
- Would you get an abortion if pregnancy would interfere with your career?
- A lot of women try to get ahead by sleeping with the boss. What do you think about that sort of thing?
- In this job, it is important to please the customer. Would you mind dating some of them if it comes to that?
- Does your husband work for this company?

Again, as I pointed out in chapter 8, you can decide for yourself what to do in this situation. If you refuse to answer, you face the prospect of not getting a job. If you choose to answer freely, on the other hand, you are accepting the fact that you are willing to work for a sexist organization that will deliberately limit your chances for success. Given that many women might actually enjoy such a prospect (as was pointed out earlier), this could easily be an acceptable choice. For others, this is a repugnant idea and they would never even consider a job with a company like this. There may be a comfortable middle ground.

Some Verbal Strategies

The following verbal strategies are designed to help the candidate deal with or prevent illegal, sexist questions:

- Avoid an emotional response. Try to remain cool and collected.
- Stick to business topics. Do not get personal. This avoids opening up personal areas of your life.
- Turn the question around and answer with a neutral, positive response.

- Use the interviewer title or last name; this promotes formality.
- Express ideas and facts, not feelings.

The following nonverbal strategies are also designed to help the candidate deal with or prevent illegal, sexist questions:

- Dress formally and conservatively. This promotes a more formal, less personal atmosphere.
- Maintain eye-contact. Men are impressed, even threatened by strong eye-contact from women.
- Shake hands firmly, with confidence.
- Do not smile except during the initial greeting and when you are leaving.
- Do not let your body show that you are upset by a sexist remark or question. Maintain body control.

If you follow these general suggestions, they should help you. Still, if you decide to play the game, you must recognize that you are tacitly accepting the sexist situation.

11

Picking Up
the Pieces after
Being Fired

FOR MANY PEOPLE, THE IDEA OF BEING FIRED IS SO TERRIBLE IT IS beyond their ability to even contemplate the possibility. Yet, statistics show that being fired (forced to leave a job) is very common. Even as you read this, thousands of people across America are finding a "pink slip" in their pay envelope or are being told verbally not to return the next day. Whether the person is being let go because of a discipline process or because the company is not doing well (being laid off), the effect is essentially the same. The individual feels cheated, angry, humiliated, possibly desperate. The bottom line is that he or she is suddenly unemployed.

It is bad enough when a person is just starting out. Feelings of failure can lead to serious problems relating to self worth and self-esteem. But when the individual is an established professional in his or her field, the effect is compounded many times.

Even if the individual has been informed months in advance that he or she is being let go, thus allowing him or her time to find something else, there is still a nearly overwhelming sense of failure for most people. It is perfectly common for people in this situation to blame themselves, to engage in self-destructive behavior, and to withdraw from those around them. I know these symptoms well. I've been fired or laid off from more jobs than I care to remember.

DEALING WITH THE REJECTION AND LOSS

Before you start to look for a job, you have to feel good about yourself. To do this may take time but you must deal with your feelings of rejection and loss before going any further.

The first thing to do is recognize that you are not alone. With the increase of automation of work, the chances of being replaced by a machine are increasing at an alarming rate, and it is not just happening to blue collar workers. For example, physicians spend most of their time diagnosing patient illness, but according to many sources, those efforts often are incorrect. Scientists are now creating machines that do a much better job of diagnosing. The effect, of course, is a need for fewer physicians, a fact that is already being felt in the medical profession. As the former administrator of a group of medical clinics I can personally attest to this phenomena. How do you imagine a physician feels, when he or she knows he or she has been replaced by a machine?

Second, you must recognize that anger and bitterness, can overcome a person. When this happens, the rejected employee can lash out at the former employer to the point of losing new opportunities. For instance, the fired employee may complain about his or her last employer in an interview for a new job. Or he or she may become so obsessed with losing the job that all he or she thinks about is telling the world how he or she was abused. In any case, he or she must come to grips with the situation before he or she looks for a new position.

One important part of this transition is for you to continue to do the same things and live the same way you did before you were fired or laid off; psychologists are clear on this point. Although, given the financial realities of the situation, you may have to scale down your lifestyle a bit. The more you change your behavior and pattern of living, the more you will reinforce the negative feelings you have about your predicament through denying yourself this or that and then blaming your former employer. By the same token, not significantly changing your lifestyle reinforces the idea that things are not so bad and that you can look to the future with optimism.

ASSESSING STRENGTHS

At this point, you must recognize your own assets. This step is imperative before you begin a job search. If you do not think you have value, who will? It becomes a matter of sitting down and recognizing strengths and weaknesses. There are strong indications that it is best to write out a list in the following fashion:

Strengths	Weaknesses
• highly skilled	• impatient
• very friendly	• careless
• hard working	• reactionary
• risk taker	• demanding
• dependable	• too serious
• considerate	
• helpful	
• thorough	
• broad experience	

A list of this sort should reflect the candidate's real feelings. Once it is finished, it should be reviewed by a friend who can give you additional input and clarification. This may seem like a mechanical exercise but it works because it focuses on your value as an employee, while it also shows you what you need to work on.

FOCUSING YOUR JOB SEARCH

Now that you feel better about yourself and understand yourself a little more, you should begin to focus on what you want to do. Is this the time for a career change or should you stick with your present occupation or profession? (In chapter 8 we discussed the job-changing process.) Whatever the answer is to this question, the candidate should look at the situation as a challenge to get involved in bigger and better things. This will aid your job search a great deal because it will increase your sensitivity to the opportunities out there.

DEALING WITH YOUR INCOME NEEDS

Now comes the tough part. It is all well and good to look into new possibilities; but, the candidate must be realistic when it comes to financial matters. How much money do you really need every month to pay all the bills and live the way you want to? (Remember, you want to continue to live as you have in the past for emotional and psychological reasons.)

You should begin by doing a careful inventory of your financial assets such as bank accounts, stocks, property, etc. Next, determine what your current liabilities are, including mortgages, automobile loans, and credit card payments. After you have done all of this, you must also average your daily living expenses such as utilities, food, entertainment, and clothing. The final step is calculating where your assets can help and what your financial needs are. If you do this carefully, you are in a position to know what your minimum income level is, so that when you are offered a job, you know what you can and cannot accept. It will also tell you how long you can afford to be out of work.

If this analysis tells you that you must find work in a hurry to avoid losing your automobile, it may be a question of taking a low-paying night time job just to make ends meet. But this should not be an end in itself. This strategy serves two ends. First, it gives you the necessary income to avoid a loss. Second, it allows you to continue to job-search during the day. Incidentally, there is no need to mention to a prospective employer that you have taken this night job that is below your experience and educational level. In fact, it might bias your case. In any event, taking a temporary job that permits you to gain some income while freeing you to continue to look for the right position should be seen as a stepping stone to new employment that will satisfy your real needs.

Above all, try to avoid selling things off and giving things up if at all possible. Such actions can depress you and make you bitter.

12

Dealing with
the Unexpected

NO MATTER HOW HARD YOU TRY TO PLAN YOUR JOB SEARCH, THERE
are always things that can go wrong. This chapter is a brief effort to
alert you to some typical, potential problems you may face.

THE SHAM INTERVIEW

Believe it or not, the chances are very high that at some time you
will be involved in an interview that is being carried out with no
intention of hiring any of the applicants. Occasionally, it is a question of the organization going through the motions to satisfy some
legal requirement (e.g. E.E.O.) without any real commitment to
employing anyone. Or it may be a case of the interviewer having
already made up his or her mind. Perhaps the interviewer is conducting the interview to be polite, or maybe his or her superior has
demanded that he or she talk to a certain number of people. Whatever the reason for the sham, there is little you can do to get the
job because there was no question of hiring you in the first place.

About the most you can do in this situation is to try to discover
if this is really the case and act accordingly. For one thing, you
won't have false hopes about the job. For another, you can relax
and use the interview as a practice session. The trick, of course, is
finding out if the interview is genuine.

One way to decide this is to listen to what the interviewer
says, or doesn't say. In my experience, the individual will give him

or herself away by speaking in gross generalities; refusing to answer questions directly, in detail; and, making negative asides about the job and/or the organization itself.

Another clue to the deception can be seen in the way the interviewer acts. As was indicated earlier, contemporary research in nonverbal communication tells that people give themselves away when they lie. Arms folded across the chest, a hand placed against the face while talking to you, averted eye-contact during discussion about the position; these are all clear indications that either the interviewer is lying outright or holding something back.

The best advice about the sham interview is to rely on your instincts. If something doesn't seem right, listen carefully and watch the employer. Sooner or later he or she will give him or herself away.

THE ROUND ROBIN INTERVIEW

As often as not, employers do not tell you that you are going to be interviewed by a number of people during one visit. Either they forget or they deliberately don't tell you so that you can't prepare for this type of situation.

As was suggested in chapter 3, the round robin interview isn't really much of a threat if you are truly prepared; but, it can be unsettling if you don't expect it.

One of the most important things to remember about this type of interview is to be consistent in your answers. Whatever you tell one interviewer you must tell the other. If you contradict yourself you will be perceived as confused or lying, and your credibility will slip proportionately.

Another thing to remember is that you must stress your good points more emphatically than you normally would. This is because you want all of the interviewers to agree on your main strengths. As it is, there will be a significant difference of opinion about you from one interviewer to another, so it is your job to minimize that difference.

THE GROUP INTERVIEW

From time to time you may find yourself in a situation where you are unexpectedly being interviewed by a number of people at the same time. Usually, employers do this because the candidate will be working with, or for, all of the interviewers, or each of the interviewers has an area of expertise that he or she will ask questions about.

The first thing you must do is find out who the "leader" is and make a special effort to please him or her by taking extra time to answer his or her questions and agreeing with everything he or she says. Occasionally, you will be told who this person is; at other times you will have to figure it out for yourself. One clue to determining who is the leader, is who speaks first to introduce the others, or to explain the interview situation. Another clue is, who the others defer to when several people begin to speak at the same time; still another, is who controls the flow of questions.

Once you have located the leader it is time to seek out a friendly face; someone who seems empathetic. It is important to find this person because he or she is the one who may be able to swing the others to support you for the position. Once you have found him or her try to cultivate the individual by directing answers to him or her and confirming anything he or she says.

It is possible that there will not be a "friendly" or particularly supportive interviewer in the group but that would be very rare. It is my experience that there is always someone who seems more understanding or interested than the others. Again, your chances of getting the job may well rest in the hands of that one person.

THE ILLEGAL QUESTIONS

Despite Federal and state laws, interviewers will often ask questions that are against the law to ask. These include inquiries into the sex of the applicant, marital status, age, religion, race, color of skin, hair, or eyes, arrests, relatives, dependents, birthplace, national origin, and even whether or not you rent or own a home. In fact, many of the application forms you will be asked to fill out will ask these questions. The following is a list of legal and illegal questions that you might be asked.

Legal	Illegal
1. Have you ever worked for this company before using a different name?	1. Is your name Polish?
2. Do you live within a 50 mile radius of the plant?	2. Where do you come from, Germany?

3. Do you believe you are strong enough to do this job?

3. Do you think that this job is appropriate for a woman?

4. Would you feel comfortable working for this organization?

4. How do you feel about working for a Baptist college?

5. Where did you go to college?

5. Isn't Howard University a black college?

6. Are you an American citizen?

6. Are you a native-born American?

7. Do you have a state work permit issued by your school?

7. You look about 30 years old. Am I right?

8. Can you speak French?

8. Is French your native tongue?

9. Can we have a photograph of you *after* you are hired?

9. Can I have a photograph of you to show to the boss?

10. Can we have the name of a person to notify in case of an emergency?

10. Is this person you have listed for emergencies your wife?

11. Are you an officer in the Coastal Club?

11. Isn't the Coastal Club a male-only organization?

12. Have you served in the U.S. Armed Forces?

12. Were you honorably discharged?

13. Would you be willing to work the second shift?

13. Would you be willing to work on Christmas Day?

14. Are you continuing to go to college?

14. Did you ever study accounting, not that it really matters?

15. Can we have the name of three work references?

15. Can we contact your minister for a reference?

16. How many years experience do you have as a welder?

16. Did you ever work for the Ajax company as a welder?

17. Are you bondable?

17. What kind of credit rating do you have?

18. Is there anything in your non-professional life which might interfere with your ability to do this job?

18. Are you married?

19. Do you have any sort of handicap that might interfere with your ability to do this job?

19. Have you ever been in a mental institution?

20. Have you ever been convicted of a crime?

20. Have you ever been arrested?

When you are asked these illegal questions, you have only two choices. If you want the job, you will have to answer them. If your integrity or sense of privacy prevents this, you can refuse to answer but you will probably not be hired. Technically, the employer cannot refuse to hire you because you won't answer an illegal question, but it is hard to prove that he denied you the job because of that. Incidentally, you can always report the employer to the authorities for asking such questions or take him or her to court.

Still, if you want the job you must figure out a way to answer that protects your interests while satisfying the employer. The simplest answer is to be as general as possible. For example, if he or she asks you if you plan to get married and have children, instead of saying "Yes," you can say "I'm not at all certain about that. My highest priority, at this point, is my career." Or, if he or she asks how much you weigh, you can always respond, "I'm not certain. I don't have a scale at home."

However, it may be that the only way to answer an illegal question is by distorting the truth. Although you may find this prospect troublesome, you are being put in a very unfair and illegal position and you have a right to protect yourself. If the employer asks, "How old are you?" you might increase or decrease your actual age depending on what you think is best as long as you don't break the law yourself.

HIGH PRESSURE QUESTIONS

There are those who believe that putting an interviewee under pressure is good because it tends to "bring out the real person." In other words, they maintain that what you do and say under pressure is a strong indication of what you are really like and what you really think. They also assume that if you can handle yourself under pressure, you will do that much better under ordinary business circumstances. Whether any of this thinking is accurate or not, it is not uncommon to find yourself in this situation.

The high pressure interview is designed to get you to answer very spontaneously and demands responses to difficult questions. Frequently, the interviewer shows no signs of emotion and fires the questions at you at a very fast pace. The moment you finish answering one question, he or she hits you with another.

The first thing to do in a high pressure interview is to remember that, in a very significant way, you are in charge. The interviewer wants something from you, and you can control how you respond and what information you give him or her. Accordingly, you must take your time with your answers and avoid the temptation to say the first thing that comes into your mind.

Second, remember that the pressure is only there if you decide to let it be. If the employer throws one question at you after another, with hardly a moments hesitation, you are not obligated to match that pace. In fact, the pressure is really on the interviewer in this situation, because he or she is the one who is trying to exert it.

To summarize, your best response to high pressure interviews is to take your time and try to recall your prepared answers. Whatever you do, remain as calm as possible, and recognize that you are really in the driver's seat.

THE HOSTILE INTERVIEWER

There are any number of reasons that an interviewer might be hostile toward you. It may be that he or she has simply had a bad day. Perhaps he or she was forced to do the interview in place of someone else and has other work to do. Or maybe he or she just hates to interview people. The reason for the interviewer's hostility, however, is less important than your ability to deal with it effectively.

One way to deal with the hostile interviewer is to respond in kind; to become equally hostile and tell the employer what you think of him or her. You can do that if you want, but you certainly won't get the job.

A more effective technique is to act pleasantly, even if you don't particularly feel like it. If he or she says, "This application isn't very neat!", a useful response would be to say with a smile, "I was so interested in answering everything in as much detail as possible, I guess I didn't pay much attention to style."

Or you can act the role of the understanding friend. If the interviewer claims that he or she has a very tight schedule, you can tell him how much you appreciate his or her willingness to talk to you.

Finally, if he or she goes so far as to question your honesty, you can explain with a smile that your memory isn't perfect but that your answer is based on your best recollection.

No doubt there are people who cannot respond well to this sort of petty tyranny. So it becomes a question of trying to make the best of a bad situation or engaging in an argument. It is a matter of doing what suits you best.

THE SURPRISE TEST

It won't happen very often but occasionally you will be faced with an unexpected psychological, aptitude, vocational, or technical test or exam. There is little you can do to prepare for these tests, but you can do your best if you just relax and answer honestly. Second guessing and distorting answers will only get you in trouble.

If the test is worth anything at all, it will be able to discriminate between those who are honest or really know what they are doing and those who are lying or trying to please the employer at the expense of reality.

If you feel particularly vulnerable or inadequate at that moment, you can always ask to take the test at another time. You might indicate that you are scheduled to be somewhere else in an hour, or that you don't think that you will do your best at this particular time. You can also simply refuse to take the test on the basis that you did not expect that this would be a condition of employment.

The best advice is not to put it off because refusal or reluctance to take the test may automatically disqualify you.

THE IMMEDIATE OFFER

From time to time, an overly enthusiastic employer may offer you the job on the spot. It may be very tempting to accept such an offer immediately, but that would probably be a mistake in most instances.

Anybody that anxious to offer you a job should clearly be held suspect. You should ask yourself just why is he or she so anxious. Is it because no one else wants it? Or maybe he or she hasn't told you the complete story and doesn't want you to find out the truth before you accept. Or perhaps the interviewer is untrained and inexperienced. In such situations, it is not unusual for the employer to jump the gun and offer the job to the first acceptable candidate who comes along. From his or her point of view, it may be a quick solution to a difficult problem. No matter what the reason for the employer's behavior, to accept the offer without due consideration is generally a mistake and both parties lose.

The candidate loses in that he or she may accept a job that he or she really doesn't want because of a momentary enthusiasm that can easily overshadow the realities of the situation.

The employer loses because studies show that the rate of turnover with immediate hires is substantially greater than normal. Employees either get fired because they can't do the job expected of them, or they quit because they are disappointed with the job. And when you consider that it costs thousands of dollars to hire and train a single new employee, the employer's loss is significant.

NEW AND UNACCEPTABLE CONDITIONS

Sometime in your job search you may encounter a situation similar to this: you are offered a job over the phone a few days after the interview has taken place. You accept the offer but when you show up to start work you are told that: (1) the job pays less than they originally told you; (2) you must work overtime on a routine basis; (3) the first week is training and you won't be paid for it; or (4) they have decided that they need you in a different department doing work that you hate, etc.. Such occurrences are not at all unusual. In the retail business this is known as "Switch and Bait" (advertising one thing and when the customer shows up, selling him or her something else).

As a rule, employer strategies of this sort are very deliberate and designed to intimidate you. The employer knows that you have either quit your old job or that you have set your mind on working for his or her company. Rather than having no job at all or losing this opportunity to work for the company, you will probably feel compelled to accept the new conditions. There are times when this will seem to be the only thing you can do. But bear in mind that this is a very poor way to begin a new job and the chances are very high that it won't work out. If you do accept the job, the best advice I can give, is to put the matter behind you.

13

Some Final
Words of Advice

Now, as you are prepared to begin your job search, here are some final pieces of advice.

ALWAYS ASSUME YOU CAN
HAVE THE JOB IF YOU WANT IT

If you approach the job interview with this frame of mind, you improve your chances of landing the position. That is not to say that you should be unduly arrogant; but, a strong sense of self-confidence can go a long way toward convincing the employer that you are the person for the job.

People want to hire confident people; by the same token, they avoid hiring people who seem nervous, defensive, and self-deprecating. The more you look and sound like you can do the job, the more likely it is you will get the job.

YOU ARE ULTIMATELY IN CHARGE

The employer is the customer and you are the salesperson. Although you must please the employer to get the job, as was indicated in chapter 1, you are in charge because you alone decide what you are willing to do to get the job.

Therefore, it becomes a question of taking charge of the situation without being overly aggressive. One way you can do this is to decide what accommodations you will make to get the job; what terms you are willing to accept to get the job; under what conditions you are willing to work; and how far you will go to impress the employer. Another way is to ask questions of the employer that get at points he or she has left unclear.

YOU MAY BE TOO QUALIFIED

Once, when I was applying for a job as a manager at a mid-sized financial services organization, the interviewer told me that he was very impressed with my background. He was impressed, he said, that he could not and would not hire me.

"I'm afraid the job wouldn't be challenging enough for a person with your education and experience," he commented.

"It sounds very challenging to me," I insisted. The fact was that I really wanted the job.

"No, no," he went on, "I don't think that we can take that chance. I really wish we could hire you, but it's just impossible."

With that comment he dismissed me saying that he certainly wished I wasn't so "damned over-qualified."

I was quietly outraged and I left the office without saying a word.

It is difficult for any candidate to accept the fact that he or she is not hired because he or she is too good. It is a sad sort of irony that promotes anger and frustration, but it is also a fact of life.

Now, to some extent, you have some control in this area. For example, if you think that you may be over-qualified, you can minimize certain aspects of your background in your resume. Or, in the interview itself, you can play down certain skills or experiences during the conversation. The bottom line is that it is up to you to decide what you want to reveal.

BE PERSISTENT

Job hunting can be very irritating and disappointing. There is nothing more humiliating than being told you are somehow inappropriate, not right for the job, when you know deep inside yourself that you could do the job without any difficulty. However, as has been indicated throughout this book, most of the people who hire employees for companies in this country do not know what they are doing. So there is no point in taking their judgements too seriously.

The one sure way to overcome the odds and land the job you want is to be persistent. The more often you interview, the better your chances are. It may be difficult to pick yourself up, one interview after another, and keep on trying, but believe me, it will eventually pay off.

EXPECT REJECTION

Obviously, the more you expose yourself to interviews, the more likely you are to be rejected. One study indicated that the typical job candidate is rejected five times after being interviewed before he or she lands a job.

As was indicated above, you would be wise not to take such rejection seriously. The interviewers are frequently so whimsical and bizarre in their subjective judgements, you could be Leonardo da Vinci applying for a job as a magazine illustrator and still not be hired! Rejection is just part of the process and it is only as painful as you let it be.

TRY NETWORKING

Believe it or not, the best jobs are seldom advertised in the paper or made available through employment agencies; they are filled through the networking process.

One kind of networking is to join a professional organization that offers the individual the opportunity to meet people in a particular field. For instance, if you want a job as a purchasing manager, you should join the Purchasing Managers Association of America. At their meetings you will meet those who are employed in the field and they are bound to know where the jobs are. In many cases, they will also be the people who either do the hiring or make significant recommendations to those that do.

Friends tend to hire friends. When a job becomes available, you will be given special consideration. Such an arrangement, however unscientific the process may be, is a standard way of filling positions.

The simplest way to network yourself is to find out the names of the professional or business organizations appropriate to your employment interests and join them. They can be found through professionals already in the field, through your local library, in the phone book, through college placement services, through the research department of local newspapers, and through the local chamber of commerce.

TAKE A JOB AS A STEPPING STONE

We would all like to start out at the top. Unfortunately, that is not possible or probable. More often, it is a question of working your way up.

On the other hand, there are countless low-end jobs that can give you the opportunity to: a) observe those who are in the job you want and gain a clear understanding of what they do and how they got there; b) put yourself in a position to learn and practice the skills and traits needed to do the job; and c) make yourself noticeable as the next logical choice when the position you want becomes available.

If you want a job as an advertising executive, you may have to begin in the layout department. Once you learn the field you are much more valuable to the organization and therefore much more promotable. But even if that does not work you can always go to another advertising firm at a higher level than at the company you just left. The trick is getting started in the first place so don't set your sights too high, particularly if you don't have much practical experience in the field.

IGNORE THE OLD WIVES' TALES

There is an awful lot of bad advice out there about how to land a job. For example, some people will tell you to "just be natural in the interview." As we have already discussed, this is terrible advice given that there is nothing natural about a job interview; it is a game that demands skill, not naturalness.

There are those who claim that skill and experience will win out everytime, yet nothing could be further from the truth. More often than not, decisions to hire or not hire are based on the subjective feelings of the interviewer. It is the impression you make or the friends that you have that will determine whether or not you are hired.

If you simply follow the advice in this book and ignore the nonsense from well-meaning but uninformed friends and mentors, you will be light years ahead of the competition and those who do the hiring.

TEST YOUR INTERVIEW SKILLS

It is always a good idea to test a newly acquired skill before you use it in any important situation. Consequently, it is recommended that you try out your interviewing skill on a friend or relative and ask them to rate you on your responses to the questions posed in chapters 6 and 10.

You should ask them to be as candid as possible since anything less than honesty won't help you understand your basic strengths and weaknesses. Of course, unless you know your strong points you cannot maximize them, and unless you know your weak points you cannot minimize them.

WHEN TO USE AN EMPLOYMENT AGENCY

As was pointed out earlier, using an employment agency will some-times work. There are certain companies that rely almost entirely on employment agencies for new personnel. To such companies these agencies offer many advantages. For one thing, they do all the screening work and weed out the apparently unqualified. For another, they can be scapegoated if things don't turn out well.

The other side of the coin is that these agencies have a signifi-cant and vested interest in seeing their candidates placed in the jobs that they send them to. Everytime they place someone, they get paid by the employer or candidate. So they are hardly a trust-worthy source of good personnel.

My advice is that you should use employment agencies only under two conditions: when you know that a particular agency has a lock on employment with a certain company; or, when you know that an agency regularly and successfully places people in your cho-sen field.

Unless you are aware of what you are doing, agencies can be a waste of valuable time. Therefore, if you choose to use an agency, research it carefully.

HOW TO ACCEPT A JOB OFFER

Once the employer offers you the job, there are certain things you will naturally want to know such as your compensation, benefits, and working conditions. While it is only common sense to ask about these things, do so with care because if you are not diplo-matic about such matters, you can lose a job before you get it.

Perhaps an illustration will help. I once offered a job to a woman who immediately asked about sick days and vacation time. When I answered her she then began to tell me that she "had to have the first two weeks in July off" and that "she assumed her sick days were cumulative and could be treated like vacation time." From my perspective, she seemed more interested in sick time and vacations than in the job itself, so I withdrew my offer and hired someone else.

REMEMBER IT IS A GAME

Like any game, employment interviewing is a question of knowing the rules and the skills required, and mastering both. If you play the game well, you will win; if not you will lose, no matter how qualified and experienced you are.

The important thing to remember is that anyone with average intelligence can beat the system if they rehearse their responses and understand the haphazard nature of the employment process.

A FINAL WORD OF ENCOURAGEMENT

There will be disappointments along the way. Jobs will come up that will be given to other people. But, if my personal experience is of any value at all, it has taught me that you can get the job that you want if you know how to go about it.

Good luck!

Index